A Wealth of
Common Sense

Since 1996, Bloomberg Press has published books for financial professionals, as well as books of general interest in investing, economics, current affairs, and policy affecting investors and business people. Titles are written by well-known practitioners, BLOOMBERG NEWS® reporters and columnists, and other leading authorities and journalists. Bloomberg Press books have been translated into more than 20 languages.

For a list of available titles, please visit our website at www.wiley.com/go/bloombergpress.

A Wealth of Common Sense

WHY SIMPLICITY TRUMPS COMPLEXITY IN ANY INVESTMENT PLAN

Ben Carlson

MIX
Paper from
responsible sources
FSC www.fsc.org   FSC® C005928

For Cortney and Libby, who make me smile every single day.

Contents

Introduction: Why Simplicity Is the New Sophistication

In 1776, Thomas Paine, a political activist, philosopher, and poet published a simple pamphlet that likely altered history as we know it. The title of his publication was plain and simple—*Common Sense*. This tiny pamphlet, which numbered less than 90 pages, inspired the original 13 colonies to seek their independence from Great Britain and form the United States of America. It's been said that virtually every rebel read, or at least listened to, the words written by Paine. This was Paine's introduction to *Common Sense*:

> In the following pages I offer nothing more than simple facts, plain arguments, and common sense; and have no other preliminaries to settle with the reader, than that he will divest himself of prejudice and prepossession, and suffer his reason and his feelings to determine for themselves; that he will put ON, or rather that he will not put OFF, the true character of a man, and generously enlarge his views beyond the present day.[1]

Paine's simple words ignited the people of that day to fight for their independence. As John Quincy Adams, the second president of the United States, once said, "Without the pen of the author of *Common Sense*, the sword of Washington would have been raised in vain." Paine's plain, common sense arguments provided the motivation that was so desperately needed to unite people from all walks of life to stand together in their cause. So why did Paine's words resonate with so many people? In a word—simplicity. Many writers of that day and age used dense philosophy and Latin to get their point across. Paine made his case for the benefits of independence by using clear, concise language that everyone could understand. *Common Sense* worked well with the crowds in the taverns, but was sophisticated enough to be given credibility by the Colonial dignitaries.[2]

His words lived up to the title, as common sense works on a number of levels.

Improving long-term investment results by bridging the gap between sophistication and simplicity is the point of this book. Much of the financial advice out there these days might as well be written in Latin because it comes across as another language to most investors. The financial crisis from 2007 to 2009 left some lasting scars on investors' psyches. Many don't know how to proceed or whom to trust. My goal with this book is to provide a resource that helps all investors make more informed decisions using simplicity and common sense, two things that are severely lacking in the financial industry, as a guiding framework to help alleviate some of the lasting damage from the market crash. There is an assumption that complex systems such as financial markets must require complex investment strategies and organizations to succeed. This is a false premise that far too many both inside and outside of the industry have come to believe. Most of the advice out there these days works against investors and their goals because those giving it don't have an understanding of the needs and desires of their audience.

I've spent my entire career working in portfolio management. This experience has taught me that less is always more when making investment decisions. Simplicity trumps complexity. Conventional gives you much better odds than exotic. A long-term process is more important than short-term outcomes. And perspective goes much further than tactics. Tactics are useless to investors in a matter of days—sometimes in a matter of hours. But perspective is something that stays with the investor for a lifetime. It allows you to adapt to the changing market and economic landscape. While keeping it simple won't make it any easier to predict the future—no one has a crystal ball—it can give you the necessary capacity to make rational decisions, no matter what happens next.

There are two working definitions of perspective and both apply to making better financial decisions:

1. Context: A sense of the larger picture of the world, not just what is immediately in front of us.
2. Framing: An individual's unique way of looking at the world, a way that interprets its events.[3]

Perspective is so important because, without it, even the most intelligent of investors can be ruined from a lack of self-awareness in their own abilities. Investors that fail to put the news or market moves into the proper context in regards to their own personal circumstances are fighting an uphill battle. And how you frame the world around you determines how certain events will affect your reactions to outside factors that can impact your financial decisions. Combining a lack of context with a misinformed view of the way the world works is a sure path to failure with a portfolio of investments in the financial markets. A proper perspective can give the investor the right frame of mind to be able to ignore news headlines and avoid acting on the damaging emotions that can hurt the decision-making process.

I'm not here to sell you a pot of gold at the end of a rainbow. I can't offer you a secret get-rich-quick formula for making millions of dollars overnight. The real secret is that there is no secret to be able to make millions of dollars overnight. It only happens over a period of time. Building wealth takes patience. You can't be in a hurry. Fred Schwed, a financial writer who worked on Wall Street during the Great Depression, once said, "Speculation is an effort, probably unsuccessful, to turn a little money into a lot. Investment is an effort, which should be successful, to prevent a lot of money from becoming a little."

The financial markets are like any other marketplace that brings together buyers and sellers looking to find and create value. If you understand how the markets work, and more importantly how the human brain works, the results over time can be impressive. The process does not have to be based on degree of difficulty. The goal is to gain financial independence, pay for your child's college education, go on more vacations, have more time to do what you love, or whatever your needs and desires may be. Remember, the markets are not just about building wealth and making money. They're a tool for your desires about creating freedom, time, memories, and peace of mind. These things are all attainable, as long as you have a plan in place and are able to get out of your own way.

Complexity tends to be the default option that gets used to persuade investors to buy unnecessary investment products while the vast majority of people really just need to understand more conventional options to succeed. Working with the most sophisticated portfolio strategies over the past decade has given me the ability to interpret the issues that investors should actually pay attention to as opposed to those that are used as an illusion of intelligence and control.

Noise

The information available to everyone on the planet is growing at an exponential rate. Anyone with a smartphone today has better mobile phone capabilities than the president of the United States did 25 years ago. We have better access to information than the president had 15 years ago.[4] We now have an unprecedented amount of information at our fingertips anytime we want it. There's up-to-the-minute, 24-hour news coverage. We can communicate with anyone we want no matter where they live through e-mail or social media at the click of a button. Every financial market from around the globe can be followed on a tick-by-tick basis. We can now trade stocks on our smartphones. There's no way to escape the deluge of news and financial information that the media throws at you.

Nobel Prize–winning psychologist Daniel Kahneman showed in his research that because of a bias called the affect heuristic, the human brain is very quick to make judgments and decisions based on intuitive feelings that require little thought or deliberation. The sheer amount of information available today makes it easier than ever to use these quick hunches to tell us how to act. There are times when this type of response can work in your favor, but investing is not one of them. Kahneman also found that there is another part of the brain that is much more effective in using a logical and deliberate process to think things through. This is the part of the brain that should be used for thoughtful, deliberate financial decisions. Kahneman says, "If there is time to reflect, slowing down is likely to be a good idea."[5]

Information flow will only continue to speed up in the future, so we have ourselves a conundrum. It will become more and more important to separate the meaningful from the meaningless as most people will be continuously trying to drink from the fire hose of information instead of focusing on the truly important areas that they can control. Researchers have shown that this illusion of control is more likely when many choices are available, there is a large amount of information available, and you have a personal stake in the outcome of the choice.[6] This is basically a description of the portfolio management process. We all like to think that more choices must be better, but as the number of choices grows, so, too, do the number of decisions and the likelihood of making a mistake.

For example, there are now over 77,000 mutual funds to choose from worldwide.[7] As the number of investment options available to investors continues to increase there is the assumption that complex approaches must be better. In fact, I will show that less is always more and trying to implement a more interesting or clever portfolio strategy is akin to threading the needle. Sure, it *can* work, but trying harder and increasing the number of decisions you make only increases the odds that you'll make a mistake.

The financial markets are a messy, complex system that is constantly evolving. But the answer to a complex system isn't necessarily a complex investment portfolio that requires constant activity. On the contrary, the best response to the complexities inherent in the markets is a portfolio management process that relies heavily on simplicity, transparency, and reduced levels of activity. One of the ultimate status symbols in the financial world is to consider yourself a sophisticated investor. This word invokes feelings of superiority and privilege. Sophistication is defined as having a great deal of experience, wisdom, and the ability to interpret complex issues. But sophistication does not mean that you have to utilize complexity, just that you understand it. Nassim Taleb explains this dynamic in his book *Antifragile:*

> A complex system, contrary to what people believe, does not require complicated systems and regulations and intricate policies. The simpler, the better. Complications lead to multiplicative chains of unanticipated effects. [. . .] Yet simplicity has been difficult to implement in modern life because it is against the spirit of a certain brand of people who seek sophistication so they can justify their profession.[8]

In his classic book, *Winning the Loser's Game,* investor and author Charles Ellis shares the tale of his two best friends. Both were at the peak of their careers in the medical field, each with a distinguished track record. The two friends agreed that there were two discoveries in the field of medicine that were far and away the most important breakthroughs in enhancing people's health and longevity—penicillin and having doctors and nurses wash their hands. Ellis concluded this story by sharing the lesson that advice doesn't have to be complicated to be good.

How Hard Can It Be?

Over the course of my career I've invested in, advised on, or performed due diligence on nearly every investment strategy, asset class, security, or product type that you could think of. You name it; I've been involved with it in some fashion. I've worked with high-net-worth individuals, low-net-worth individuals, and million- and billion-dollar institutional portfolios. One thing I can say for certain through this experience in the markets is that it is not easy being an extraordinary investor. It's quite rare and extremely difficult.

How difficult? Neurologist-turned-investor and author William Bernstein says that there are four basic abilities that all investors must possess in order to be successful: (1) An interest in the investing process, (2) math skills, (3) a firm grasp of financial history, and (4) the emotional discipline to see a plan through. Bernstein doesn't have much faith in the prospect of most investors in the pursuit of excellence; he states, "I expect no more than 10 percent of the population passes muster on each of the above counts. This suggests that as few as one person in ten thousand (10 percent to the 4th power) has the full skill set."[9]

I agree with Bernstein that there is only a very small subset of investors that have the combination of skills he lists as well as the ability to achieve extraordinary investment returns. Not only does it require intelligence, a solid investment process, and an ability to think differently than the crowd, it also requires a dose of luck in many cases. This is why the majority of investors shouldn't be shooting for extraordinary. Legendary investor Benjamin Graham once said, "To achieve satisfactory investment results is easier than most people realize; to achieve superior results is harder than it looks." This is the problem most investors face—they are in constant search of superior results but they do not have the internal wiring, time, or skillset necessary to create that type of performance. Satisfactory results can actually allow you to be above average and beat 70 to 80 percent of all other investors. And it's much easier than most assume. You first have to give up on the dream of superior performance and realize only a small fraction of investors ever actually get there. And most don't stay on top either (more on this later in the book).

The problem for average investors is that when they aim for superior results, it more often than not leads to below-average performance. It's amazing how easy it is to do worse by trying to do better. The single greatest challenge you face as an investor is handling the truth about yourself. This is why it's an unrealistic goal for the average investor to try to become the world's greatest investor. A far more worthy goal is being better than average, which is totally realistic and achievable. Better than average can lead to impressive results in terms of investment performance over long enough time horizons. It's all about harnessing the power of thinking long-term, cutting down on unforced errors, and having the patience to allow compound interest to work in your favor.

The question is: How does one go about this?

Here is some standard investment advice that is both simple and effective:

1. Think and act for the long term.
2. Ignore the noise.
3. Buy low, sell high.
4. Keep your emotions in check.
5. Don't put all of your eggs in one basket.
6. Stay the course.

These are all great pieces of advice. The question is *how*. How do I know what long term even means for me? How do I buy low and sell high? How do I keep my emotions out of the equation? How do I diversify my portfolio correctly? How do I stay the course and reduce the noise that finds its way into my portfolio? These are the questions I seek to answer throughout this book. *What* to do is not nearly as important as *how* to do it.

The biggest problem for most people is that good investment advice will always sound the best and make the most sense when looking back at the past or planning ahead for the future. It will rarely sound so great in the moment when you actually have to use it. As you will see throughout, this is both extremely simple, but maddeningly difficult at the same time. As Warren Buffett once said, "Intelligent investing is not complex, though that is far from saying it is easy."

This line sums up the point of this book very well.

Notes

1. Thomas Paine, *Common Sense* (Radford, VA: A&D Publishing, 2007).
2. Jill Lepore, "The Sharpened Quill," *The New Yorker,* October 16, 2006, www.newyorker.com/magazine/2006/10/16/the-sharpened-quill.
3. Ryan Holiday, *Obstacle Is the Way: The Timeless Art of Turning Trials into Triumph* (New York: Portfolio/Penguin, 2014).
4. Peter Diamondis, *Abundance: The Future Is Better Than You Think* (New York: Free Press, 2014).
5. Daniel Kahneman, *Thinking, Fast and Slow* (New York: Farrar, Straus, & Giroux, 2011).
6. Richard Peterson, *Inside the Investor's Brain: The Power of Mind Over Money* (Hoboken, NJ: John Wiley & Sons, 2007).
7. Investment Company Institute, *2014 Investment Company Factbook: A Review of Trends and Activities in the U.S. Investment Company Industry 54th Edition.*
8. Nassim Nicholas Taleb, *Antifragile: Things That Gain from Disorder* (New York: Random House. 2014).
9. William Bernstein, *The Investor's Manifesto: Preparing for Prosperity, Armageddon, and Everything in Between* (Hoboken, NJ: John Wiley & Sons, 2012).

A Wealth of
Common Sense

The Individual Investor versus the Institutional Investor

When "dumb" money acknowledges its limitations, it ceases to be dumb.

—Warren Buffett

I was fresh out of college and in the early days of my career in the money management industry, but I could tell this talk was a big deal. It was one of my first big industry conferences and it was standing room only. The room was packed with professional investors, portfolio managers, and consultants, all eagerly awaiting the message to be delivered by a well-known billionaire hedge fund manager. There was a buzz in the air. At every investment conference there is always one speech that every attendee circles on their agenda. This was that speech.

After taking the podium and making the customary break-the-ice joke, the headline speaker got right into his speech. It covered a wide variety of topics on the markets and the investment industry in general. It was very data driven, but interesting and even funny at times. You could tell that he had plenty of practice over the years speaking to large crowds such as this one. There were no note cards or PowerPoint slides. It was like you were having a one-on-one conversation with a business associate. Everyone around me was frantically scribbling away in their notebooks so they could look back on his words of wisdom in the future. Once the bulk of the current market outlook was through he decided to spend some time going over the big changes he foresaw in the investment management industry in the coming years.

He made the claim that many of the best, academically tested, evidence-based investment strategies from the past—once only reserved for the wealthy elite at a very high cost—would soon become available to all investors through low-cost exchange-traded funds (ETFs) and mutual funds that could be instituted on a systematic, quantitative basis. At the time ETFs were still a relatively new product, so this was somewhat of a bold call that not many were making at the time. He was predicting a sea change in the industry.

In way of background on ETFs, the industry has experienced explosive growth in assets under management in the past decade and a half. ETFs in all financial asset classes carried only $70 billion in assets in the year 2000. By the end of 2014, that number was closer to $2 trillion, an unbelievable growth trajectory.[1] For the uninitiated, an ETF is very much like a mutual fund in that it allows you to hold a number of different securities under a single fund structure. This allows investors to buy a diversified pool of securities so you don't have to buy them each individually. The biggest difference is that ETFs trade on the stock exchanges throughout the day, just like individual stocks, whereas mutual funds transactions only happen at the market close. ETFs are also structured in a way that that makes them very tax and cost efficient, so they're cheaper, on average, than mutual funds. ETFs have better transparency of their holdings than mutual funds, as you can view ETF holdings on a daily basis. They aren't nearly as affected by forced buying and selling as mutual funds can be.[2] ETFs are allowing enterprising fund companies to slice and dice risk factors, sectors, regions, and asset classes in a number of interesting ways. This should only continue in the future, as these strategies will become more and more specialized. ETFs are worth paying attention to as they will only carve out an ever-larger market share of investor dollars over time.

Back to the investment conference: I found myself nodding in agreement with this fund manager as he surgically laid out the reasoning behind the potential shift to make better investment strategies available at a lower cost to more and more investors—increased competition, availability of information, a dearth of academic studies on back-tested strategies, and the fact that most professional portfolio managers came from similar schools of thought. This was making it harder and harder for portfolio managers to justify their claims of superior investment processes at a much higher cost to the individual investor. The line of thinking was that these newer products wouldn't offer the possibility for enormous outsized gains, but at a reduced cost to the investor, would give similar returns on a net basis after costs, the only thing that really matters in the end.

When the speech was over, there was a Q&A session that gave the professional investors in the room a chance to follow up with this hedge fund manager about his speech. Participants quickly hurried to the microphones to ask this famous investor a question. The first audience member, looking a little flustered, didn't waste any time as he asked, "How are we ever supposed to sell these lower cost funds to our clients? Won't this be an admission that we're buying sub-par funds?" As I looked around the room I noticed nearly every other investor nodding their head in agreement. One by one they all took their turn asking similar questions.

"How can we justify the use of inferior funds?"

"Don't you understand that you get what you pay for?"

"How do we prove our value-add when selecting these types of funds?"

"How could we ever sell the fact that we're not buying the best of breed funds at the highest cost? We might as well admit we don't know what we're doing!"

At first, this reaction by my fellow, more experienced investors, made absolutely no sense to me. Why wouldn't they be thrilled about the fact that certain strategies would now be much more accessible at a lower cost in a more shareholder-friendly investment vehicle? Wasn't the investment industry becoming flatter and more cost-effective a good thing for advisors, consultants, and investors alike?

Then I started to realize my naiveté. I was still a rookie in the field of finance. Not everything works in black and white when it comes to products and investment choices in the financial services industry. All of the pros in the room were thinking about the same thing—signaling. If they were using inferior products at a lower cost, they would be signaling to their clients that they weren't doing their job to uncover the best investment products available in the marketplace. These investors and allocators of capital were worried about becoming marginalized. If they couldn't offer access to only *the best funds*, then how would that look to current and potential clients? If you have your name on the list at the best nightclub in the city, you're in exclusive company. But if that velvet rope is open to everyone that wants to get in, suddenly the shine comes off just a bit and you don't feel so special anymore. Also, you get what you pay for is an expensive theory, but one that all too many still believe in. It's more or less a sales tactic, but one with a narrative that's difficult to shake for many both inside and outside the industry.

It was far too counterintuitive for these investors to accept the fact that they could earn above average returns at a lower cost while giving up the opportunity for extraordinary performance at a much higher cost. The extraordinary performance was much harder to get and there was no way that all of them were going to be able to succeed in finding it, but how could they admit this fact and not even try? These are very competitive people. They all went to top colleges and universities. Most attended the top business schools, obtained the prestigious CFA designation, or both. Everyone in the room was intelligent and extremely qualified. Investing can be a cutthroat business. Everyone wants to be the best investor by making the most money possible in the shortest amount of time. Unfortunately, it's just not possible for every single professional investor to be in the top echelon of the performance rankings. This can be a difficult realization to come to.

The look on the speaker's face was priceless after he finished answering the final round of angry questions from the audience. He had a smirk on his face. It was almost like he knew what was coming for many of these investors based on their reactions. He knew it was only a matter of time before market participants came around to his line of thinking. But breaking established viewpoints on the markets can be difficult for intelligent people. It's not easy to admit that there might be another way of doing things, a simpler approach.

Luckily, individual investors don't have to worry about entrenched positions from the investment industry. You don't have to try to impress anyone. You don't have to invest in the Rolls Royce of portfolios to reach your goals. A more economical, fuel-efficient model will do the trick as long as you're not worried about impressing anyone else (which you should not be). It's about getting from point A to point B, not how you get there. There are no style points when investing. There's no bonus for degree of difficulty. You don't have to signal that you invest only in the best, most exclusive strategies. No one is there to judge you or your portfolio and you don't have to compete against your peers. The most important thing is that you increase your probability for success. That's all.

Coming to this realization can be a huge weight lifted off your shoulders because, as you'll see in the next section, being in the upper echelon of investors is nearly impossible for even the professionals that do this for a living.

Institutional versus Individual Investors

Professional investors now control the markets, but it wasn't always like this. Fifty years ago, the little guy controlled the stock market, as individuals made up more than 90 percent of trading volume on the New York Stock Exchange. Today those roles are reversed, as institutions handle more than 95 percent of all trades in listed stocks while trading almost 100 percent of all other investable securities. Institutional investors such as pension funds, endowments, foundations, sovereign wealth funds, and wealthy family offices have trillions of dollars at their disposal to invest.[3]

Warren Buffett is probably the most well-known investor to the average guy or gal on the street. Not as many individual investors know who David Swensen is. Swensen is Warren Buffett in the world of institutional money management. He's one of the greatest institutional investors of all time. Swensen literally wrote the book on the institutional investment model, called *Pioneering Portfolio Management*. They even call his style of portfolio management, which has been imitated by hundreds and hundreds of investment funds around the globe, the Yale Model, because he is the chief investment officer for the Yale University endowment fund. Swensen has earned Yale nearly 14 percent per year in gains since the mid-1990s, an unbelievable run of performance over two decades.

Yale's portfolio is currently valued at over $20 billion. For those wishing to replicate Swensen's success, it's worth noting the structure of Yale's endowment fund. The school brings in hundreds of millions of dollars a year in charitable donations and grants. Ivy leaguers love giving back to their alma maters. Yale has a staff of 26 fulltime investment professionals who specialize in particular areas of expertise for the portfolio. Plus, Yale is a tax-exempt organization, meaning they don't have to worry about tax implications when it comes to their portfolio decisions. They also have a time horizon of forever, more or less, as the endowment is a perpetuity to the school. Large institutions, such as Yale, have access to certain funds that most average investors can't invest in because the minimums are far too large. There are deals that the largest players in the industry are involved in that would never become available to individual investors. Large pools of capital get a foot in the door simply for having such so much money at their disposal. The scale of these funds allows them to pay less in fees as a percentage of assets through negotiations because the absolute amounts can be so large.

While it's important to distinguish between individual and institutional investors, Swensen is quick to point out that even within the rank of professional investors there is a hierarchy. In the Yale Investment Office's 2013 annual report, Swensen offered the following advice to both institutional and individual investors alike (emphasis mine):

> The most important distinction in the investment world does not separate individuals and institutions; the most important distinction divides those investors that have the ability to make high-quality active management decisions from those investors without active management expertise. Few institutions and even fewer individuals exhibit the ability and commit the resources to produce risk-adjusted excess returns.
>
> The correct strategies for investors with active management expertise fall on the opposite end of the spectrum from the appropriate approaches for investors without active management abilities. Aside from the obvious fact that skilled active managers face the opportunity to generate market-beating returns in traditional asset classes of domestic and foreign equity, skilled active managers enjoy the more important opportunity to create lower-risk, higher returning portfolios with the alternative asset classes, and private equity. Only those investors with active management ability sensibly pursue market-beating strategies in traditional asset classes and portfolio allocation to nontraditional asset classes.
>
> *No middle ground exists. Low-cost passive strategies suit the overwhelming number of individual and institutional investors without the time, resources, and ability to make high-quality decisions.* The framework of the Yale model applies to only a small number of

investors with the resources and temperament to pursue the grail of risk-adjusted excess returns.[4]

One of the biggest problems for individual investors just starting out is that they try to pursue the grail of earning higher returns with lower risks without the proper understanding of how hard it truly is to obtain. They assume that they need to use the most sophisticated investment strategies to succeed in the markets. On the flipside of that coin, those that are at the top of their game and have used the most complex approaches always seem to offer simple solutions to individual investors. In essence, they are saying, "Do as I say, not as I do." In a way, it takes an understanding of complexity to see the beauty in simplicity. This is a painful lesson for individuals to learn on their own, which is why it's preferable to let someone else pay the tuition for you. Learn from them and try not to make the same mistakes or understand why they advise you to think and act a certain way when investing.

The middle ground that Swensen describes is a place that many investors often find themselves stuck in. They want to try to beat the market by using sophisticated strategies, but they don't have the resources or knowhow to do it. In this case, trying to be above-average leads to below-average performance. Trying too hard becomes a weight around your neck. There's no shame in admitting that truly extraordinary market performance, such as Swensen's, is difficult to achieve. What hurts most investors is trying to be extraordinary in the markets, without the correct understanding that it's a game suited for a small number of investors.

The middle ground isn't reserved just for individual investors either. It's also littered with institutional investors that don't have the same resources or expertise as Yale. Table 1.1 shows the

Table 1.1   Endowment Fund Annual Performance Comparison

	5 Years	10 years	15 Years	20 Years	25 Years
Yale University Endowment	3.30%	11.00%	11.80%	13.50%	13.20%
Harvard University Endowment	1.70%	9.40%	9.60%	11.90%	11.50%
All Endowments	3.80%	6.80%	5.60%	7.70%	8.40%
60% Stocks, 40% Bonds	5.90%	7.40%	5.70%	7.60%	8.30%

Source: Vanguard.

performance numbers over varying time horizons for Yale's Endowment Fund along with the numbers for one of their peers, Harvard, and the record for all endowment funds set against a simple 60/40 stock/bond benchmark. These numbers show how extraordinary Swensen's long-term results have been over a multidecade time horizon—phenomenal, in fact. Harvard, one of Yale's biggest rivals, has also shown the ability to deliver above average long-term returns, as well. Now look at the results of all endowment funds in this institutional investment universe. When compared to a 60/40 portfolio made up of two simple index funds the results look nearly identical. They basically matched a balanced fund's performance over every period, not something most novice investors would expect.[5]

Not only is it difficult for the average individual investor to come close to matching David Swensen's return figures, but even his peers in the institutional investment community have a hard time coming anywhere near his performance. In fact, most have a hard time beating one of the simplest portfolios you can create for nearly nothing in fees today. Swensen himself is an advocate for passive funds; as he says, "Certainly, the game of active management entices players to enter, offering the often false hope of excess returns. Perhaps those few smart enough to recognize that passive strategies provide a superior alternative believe themselves to be smart enough to beat the market. In any event, deviations from benchmark returns represent an important source of portfolio risk."[6] This comes from a guy who has beat the market handily over the past two and a half decades. Sometimes it takes the perspective from someone that utilizes a complex approach to portfolio management to recognize the beauty of simplicity for everyone else without the same resources at their disposal.

Yale is definitely the Michael Jordan of the institutional investing world. (I guess that makes Harvard the Kobe Bryant?) It's a pipe dream to think individual investors can match their success. But look at the results of the rest of these multimillion- and billion-dollar portfolios: A simple 60/40 mix of stock and bond index funds that merely matches the returns of the market is right there over every single time frame. It's not out of the realm of possibilities for the average investor to hang with professional investment offices, assuming they have the required patience, discipline, and long-term perspective.

To match or even beat the performance of institutional investors, the individual has to think differently. You can't try to beat Wall Street at its own game. In this case, a very simple portfolio pulled in nearly the same performance with much less work involved and a far simpler strategy. Obviously, not all institutional investors can outperform the market. There will always be winners and losers.

Yet just think about all the work that goes into the returns for the institutional investors. Each large fund has a fulltime staff that can range in size from a few trained professionals to more than a couple thousand at the largest pension funds. There are also third-party consultants and back-office employees. The fulltime staffs that run these funds are constantly researching and analyzing the markets for investment opportunities. Although information access is becoming more widespread, annual budgets allow institutional investors to pay top dollar for the best research and market-data providers.

On the flipside, individual investors are on their own more often than not. If you don't work in the industry, you probably have a fulltime job or family to worry about. You can't track the markets or perform research on a daily basis. Even though your investments are extremely important to your future well-being, you have to live your life and likely don't have the time or interest to follow the markets as closely as the pros. As individuals, we are much more emotionally invested in our portfolios because it's our money. It's not other people's money that we're managing. No one's ever going to care more about your money that you. Your investment portfolio really contains your goals and desires.

We're All Human

One of the biggest mistakes investors make is letting their emotions get in the way of making intelligent investment decisions. Research shows individuals sell winning stocks and hold on to losing stocks. They chase past performance and make decisions with the herd, buying more stocks after a huge run-up in price and selling after a market crash.[7] These errors cost investors a lot of money when compounded over very long time horizons.

Even with all of the advantages outlined in the previous section, professional investors are not immune from making these same exact mistakes. Researchers looked at a dataset of more than 80,000 annual observations of institutional accounts from 1984 through 2007. These funds collectively managed trillions of dollars in assets. The study looked at the buy and sell decisions among stocks, bonds, and externally hired investment managers. The researchers found that the investments that were sold far outperformed the investments that were purchased. Instead of systematically buying low and selling high, these professional pools of money bought high and sold low. We often hear of individual investors buying and selling mutual funds at the wrong times (we'll get to that later), but this study shows that professional investors practice this same type of money-destroying behavior. In fact, the authors of the study figured that these poor decisions caused this group of investors to lose more than $170 billion.[8]

Another study looked at large pension plans. These funds had an average size of $10 billion each, but they also made the mistake of chasing past performance. Nearly 600 funds were studied from 1990 to 2011. The authors of the study found that these sophisticated funds allowed their stock allocation to drift higher when the markets were rising in the bull market of the late 1990s, making them overweight to their target asset allocation percentages. So when the market crashed they held more stocks than their policies and risk controls suggested. And following the financial crisis in 2008, these funds were far underweight in their target equity allocations and kept them low. These pension funds didn't factor in reversion to the mean. All they did was extrapolate the recent past into their current decisions. They didn't rebalance by buying low and selling high. To stay within their stated objectives they should have been trimming stocks in the late 1990s as they ran up higher and buying stocks after the crash in 2008, but that's not what happened at all. Instead they were fighting the last war and investing through the rearview mirror instead of sticking to their investment policy guidelines. Risk management was secondary to chasing returns.[9]

Why does this type of behavior exist, from professionals down to the individual? In the classic movie *Wall Street*, Michael Douglas's character Gordon Gekko famously said, "Greed, for a lack of a better word, is good."[10] And while greed is said to be a driving factor in most financial decisions, envy can actually dissuade us from reaching our goals as well. In one study, Harvard researchers asked subjects if they would rather live in a place where they had income of $50,000, but the average person had an income of $25,000 or one where they have an income of $100,000 in a place where the average income was $200,000—assuming prices were constant in both examples. In the end 52 percent of the respondents preferred the $50K salary, half as much money in absolute terms as the other option but twice as much as their neighbors.[11]

Envy finds its way into the world of institutional money management as well. One of the reasons for this is the fact that people are the ones investing these portfolios. Professional investors, although much more used to the ups and downs in the markets, can succumb to human nature just as easily as anyone else. And because of all of the advantages listed above, professional investors are expected to beat the market and their own benchmarks on a consistent basis. Even though it shouldn't matter, professional investors are constantly comparing themselves to their peers in the industry. The one-upmanship can be fierce when the annual return numbers are made public. While competition can be healthy in many aspects of life, when comparing portfolios with different goals, objectives, risk profiles, and time horizons, this type of behavior can lead to unforced errors when trying to beat your fellow investors.

Speaking of relative performance—institutional investors not only benchmark themselves against peers in the industry, but also against custom or index-based internal benchmarks. Benchmarking can be helpful in some ways for individuals (more on this later in the book), but the only benchmarks that really matter are your own personal goals. If your portfolio is able to meet those goals, who cares if you beat the market or not? You don't have to judge yourself on any particular timeframe against a set index or market. Investing doesn't have to be about beating others or beating the market. It's about not beating yourself.

These different goals are the reason investors shouldn't worry about how the professionals invest or even what type of performance numbers they're putting up on an annual basis. They say if you want to win against a team with superior talent in sports, you don't try to beat them at their own game. You level the playing field by exploiting their weaknesses and utilizing your strengths. That means trying to get involved in the increasingly competitive world of professional money management is not the game individuals should be trying to play. You're at a competitive disadvantage.

Extra Zeroes

When you work with large institutional portfolios, it can be a bit overwhelming at first. It takes some time to get used to working with market values and investments with a few extra zeroes. But after a while you realize that's all they really are, a few extra zeroes. Yes, there can be more pressure involved when you're investing multimillion- or billion-dollar portfolios. But the same basic investment principles apply to even the largest portfolios. Every investment plan and portfolio is going to be different because every individual or organization has unique circumstances and cash flow needs. But at the end of the day, those extra zeroes have to follow the same basic principles whether you're managing $10,000,000 or $10,000. There's an old saying that people don't go to church on Sundays expecting to hear an eleventh commandment. They go to reinforce the ten that are already in place. Every investor, both big and small, is forced to deal with erratic markets and an uncertain future. There's no reason to try to reinvent the wheel and come up with some exotic strategy that no one else has figured out to try to change this fact.

Having more capital to invest shouldn't shield large pools of capital from creating a comprehensive investment plan and having the discipline to follow that plan by the rules and guidelines set out by the investment policy statement. There are no short cuts.

You most likely don't have the time, experience, or expertise, to try to be an extraordinary investor on the same level as David Swensen at Yale. But it's okay to admit this fact. Those who don't are the ones who get themselves into trouble. The competition for the very best investment ideas is now higher than it's ever been. That competition is only going to get fiercer over time. Professional investors are constantly on the lookout for ways to improve their portfolios by looking at different securities, industries, markets, asset classes, geographies, investment managers, and fund structures.

Individuals have to understand that no matter what innovations we see in the financial industry, patience will always be the great equalizer in the financial markets. There's no way to arbitrage good behavior over a long time horizon. In fact, one of the biggest advantages individuals have over the pros is the ability to be patient. You don't have to answer to a committee or a group of clients. No one is judging you against your peers or a custom-made benchmark. There's no one to impress. It's not that all of the professional investors don't think for the long term; it's just much more diffi-cult to pull off for some because of the culture of comparisons and benchmarking. You can trade as little as you want and no one will be there to question your results in the short term. You can extend your time horizon for as long as your circumstances dictate and allow the magic of compound interest to do the heavy lifting for you. There's no need to worry about the next week, month, quarter, or year with your long-term capital. Individuals have the luxury of thinking—and hopefully acting—in terms of decades, an unheard of time frame on Wall Street. The ability to be patient and disciplined while extending your time horizon can be a huge advantage.

You don't have to worry about beating the market or Harvard or Yale. You just have to worry about doing enough to reach your goals. That's your true benchmark. You can focus on yourself and your own portfolio.

Long-Term Thinking

A number of years ago, in one of my first due diligence meetings on a potential investment manager, I was listening to a marketing pitch given by a portfolio manager and what he said still stands out to me to this day. As he was giving the general outline of the firm's strategy he talked about the possible alternatives to the way that they invested in stocks. The average holding period for stocks in the fund was eighteen months and they used various market-timing indicators to try to improve performance.

In the marketing material, there was a page listing the differ-ent ways in which you can outperform as a stock investor. Number one was trading opportunistically over the very short term. Number two was to find the intermediate-term trends in sectors and indus-tries and ride them before the rest of the market discovered them. Finally, number three was to be a buy and hold investor for the very long-term.

What was interesting about this presentation was that he dis-cussed the buy and hold strategy as if it were a mythical creature that could only be seen in a fairy tale. He flippantly said, "Sure, you could do very well with a buy and hold strategy but what portfolio manager has the leeway to be able to pull that off in today's environment? No investors have that kind of patience." This was crazy to me, but for the majority of investors that this portfolio manager pitched his strategy to, it was probably true. He was basically saying that none of his clients or prospective clients would give the fund a wide enough berth to pull off a buy and hold strategy because there would of course be periods where it wouldn't work. And his fund gave the apparent illusion of increasing the odds of improving upon this—even though it was probably just that, an illusion.

This isn't to say that buy and hold is a perfect strategy by any means. It's not. No strategy is perfect. But the way that this professional money manager dismissed a long-term approach simply because of impatient investors was difficult to grasp. Just because something is hard doesn't mean you shouldn't do it. The problem with a buy and hold strategy is that for it to work the way it's supposed to, you have to do both the buying and the holding during a market crash. It's much easier to both buy and hold when markets are rising. Get this right and you can be wrong in many other aspects of the investment process and still succeed. It just requires intestinal fortitude not seen in many people because we're used to running from burning buildings, not towards them.

A study performed by the Federal Reserve shows how the simplicity of a buy and hold strategy can pay dividends over the alternatives. They looked at mutual fund inflows and outflows over nearly 30 years from 1984 to 2012. Predictably, they found that most investors poured money into the markets after large gains and pulled money out after sustaining losses—a buy high, sell low debacle of a strategy. They then compared these return-chasing fund flows to a simple buy and hold strategy over seven year windows throughout the period. They found that the buy and hold strategy outperformed the return-chasing strategy by up to 5 percent per year. That means in the seven-year time frames they studied, the total return difference was as high as 40 percent in all.[12] Again, buy and hold has its flaws. Nothing works all the time or shields investors from losses. But when compared against typical investor behavior, it's not even a contest.

Another simple, yet effective way for individual investors to diversify investment decisions is through the process of dollar cost averaging (DCA) by making periodic purchases over time. This strategy ends up buying more shares at lower prices and fewer shares at higher prices. The point of dollar cost averaging isn't to perfectly time the market, but to admit that you don't have the ability or emotional control to try to time the market. Plus, rarely is it the case that investors are putting a lump sum into the market all at once. Remember, a portfolio is simply a place where you allocate your savings. Most people save a percentage of their income, making a dollar cost average strategy the most convenient way to invest, especially since the process can be automated through a workplace retirement plan. But even this strategy can be difficult to implement without the correct perspective, as Benjamin Graham pointed out when asked about DCA in the 1960s. "Such a policy will pay off ultimately, regardless of when it is begun, *provided* that it is adhered to conscientiously and courageously under all intervening conditions." But for this strategy to work out an investor must, "be a different sort of person from the rest of us . . . not subject to the alternations of exhilaration and deep gloom that have accompanied the gyrations of the stock market for generations past." Graham's conclusion, "This, I greatly doubt," says a lot about his knowledge on the emotions of investors.[13]

These are just two very basic investment ideas that are simple, but not easy, in practice. Both can work for the majority of investors as a good baseline assumption before doing a deeper dive into your own circumstances, risk profile, time horizon, and investment skills.

Also, there's a big difference between buy and hold and your personal holding period. It's impossible to have a portfolio where you never make any changes. There needs to be a balance between controlling for risk and staying out of your own way, from being overly active and mistiming the market. A patient, disciplined, long-term strategy isn't easy because most of the time it requires you, the investor, to basically sit on your hands and do nothing. This may sound easy, but for many doing something, *anything*, is much easier because it gives you the feeling of control. When you make constant changes to your portfolio that activity makes you feel as if you are having an impact by not sitting still and doing nothing by following your plan.

In most areas of our lives, trying harder is great advice. But trying harder does not mean doing better in the financial markets. In fact, trying harder is probably one of the easiest ways to achieve below average performance. Reaching for superior performance over every single shortened time frame will most likely lead to worse results than accepting what the market gives you, keeping your costs low, and trying to behave. It's easy to assume that the most skilled will become the best performers in various professions. This is generally how it works out in professional sports. But it is not only the most skilled; it is also those who work the hardest. The best people should do well year after year and this is exactly how many think that the financial markets should work. Somehow this never works out in reality. There's a constant stream of intelligent people making huge mistakes in the financial markets. In the next chapter we'll look at ways to reduce these mistakes and how to improve your performance by learning from some of the greatest investors of all time.

Key Takeaways from Chapter 1

- Don't try to beat the professionals at their own game. You're at a competitive disadvantage. The greatest equalizer in the markets will always be patience. You can't arbitrage good, long-term behavior.
- Envy is perhaps the worst emotion that you can feel as an investor. It can only lead to problems. There's no logical reason to compare yourself to other investors—institutional or individual. Focus on your own situation.
- The basic investment principles apply to all investors, regardless of the size of their portfolio. The hard part is following them when those around you cannot.

Notes

1. Elisabeth Kashner, "Your ETF Has DRIP Drag," ETF.com, October 21, 2014, www.etf.com/sections/blog/23595-your-etf-has-drip-drag.html.
2. Blackrock, "ETP Landscape. Industry Highlights," September 2014, www.blackrockinternational.com/content/groups/internationalsite/documents/literature/etfl_industryhilight_sep14.pdf.
3. Charles D. Ellis, "The Rise and Fall of Performance Investing," *Financial Analysts Journal* 70, no. 4 (2014), www.cfapubs.org/doi/pdf/10.2469/faj.v70.n4.4.
4. David Swensen, "The Yale Endowment: 2013," http://investments.yale.edu/images/documents/Yale_Endowment_13.pdf.
5. Daniel W. Wallick, Brian R. Wimmer, and James J. Balsamo, "Assessing Endowment Performance: The Enduring Role of Low-Cost Investing," Vanguard, September 2014, https://institutional.vanguard.com/VGApp/iip/site/institutional/researchcommentary/article/InvResEndowPerf.
6. David Swensen, *Pioneering Portfolio Management: An Unconventional Approach To Institutional Investment* (New York: Free Press, 2000).

7. Brad Barber and Terrance Odean, "The Behavior of Individual Investors," *Haas School of Business* (September 2011).
8. Scott D. Stewart, John J. Neumann, Christopher R. Knittel, & Jeffrey Heisler, "Absence of Value: An Analysis of Investment Allocation Decisions by Institutional Plan Sponsors," *Financial Analysts Journal* 65, no. 6 (2009).
9. Andrew Ang, Amit Goyal, & Antii Ilmanen, "Asset Allocation and Bad Habits," April 2014, www.rijpm.com/pre_reading_files/Goyal _Asset_Allocation_and_Bad_Habits1.pdf.
10. Oliver Stone, *Wall Street*, Movie, Twentieth Century Fox, 1987.
11. Richard Peterson, *Inside the Investor's Brain: The Power of Mind Over Money* (Hoboken, NJ: John Wiley & Sons, 2007).
12. Federal Reserve Bank of St. Louis, "The Cost of Chasing Returns," The St. Louis Fed, September 2014, www.stlouisfed.org/on-the-economy/the-cost-of-chasing-returns/.
13. Jason Zweig, "If You Think Worst Is Over, Take Benjamin Graham's Advice," *Wall Street Journal*, May 26, 2009, http://online.wsj.com/articles/SB124302634866648217.

2

Negative Knowledge and the Traits Required to Be a Successful Investor

If you can get good at destroying your own wrong ideas, that is a great gift.

—Charlie Munger

Confucius once said, "Real knowledge is to know the extent of one's ignorance." While most investing books focus exclusively on the steps you need to take to get rich in a hurry, I'm going to start off by going the other way with some negative knowledge. Negative knowledge is the process of first looking at what does not work to eventually come to the realization of what does. This process of elimination may seem like a minor distinction and a backwards way of looking at the world, but once investors are able to negate bad behavior, all that's left over are improvements and better decisions. Negative knowledge can be much more powerful than positive knowledge because cutting down on unforced errors is so often the most important determining factor of portfolio results. It's impossible to quantify opportunity costs, but most of the best investment decisions you will ever make will be the opportunities you turn down.

The very best investors know how to stay out of their own way. This doesn't mean that every decision you make will be the correct one at the right time. That's an impossible goal. But make enough good decisions over time and reduce enough unforced errors and your probability for success is much higher than the alternative.

Why focus on negative knowledge? Because study after study shows that investor performance suffers from some very basic mistakes that should be relatively easy to fix. Investors pour money into the market at the top and pull their money out at the bottom, which has been shown to lead to an average loss of 2 percent per year in market gains. Increased trading activity from overconfidence can lead to another 1.5 to 6.5 percent in relative losses.[1] These two issues alone could cost investors an entire year's worth of market gains. One study looked at the brokerage data of individual investors to discover the 10 most important measures of poor investor behavior. They found that simply correcting these errors could improve individual investor returns by up to 3 to 4 percent per year.[2] Think about it this way— the difference between a 4 percent annual return and an 8 percent annual return over 20 years on an initial investment of $100,000 is almost $250,000, just from correcting simple mistakes.

It can be very difficult to fix the simple mistakes though, because while it's very easy to see the mistakes and biases in others, rarely do we notice them in ourselves. Figuring out where others consistently go wrong is one of the best ways to ensure your own success. With that in mind, here are seven of the biggest mistakes that investors make on a regular basis that you can put in your negative knowledge file to try to reduce or eliminate.

1. **Looking to get rich in a hurry.**

   The worst part about successful investing is that it's relatively boring. Most people are thrill seekers and would rather find their proverbial lottery ticket than have to put in the work to get rich slowly. Wouldn't life be much easier if that get-rich-quick scheme that seems like it has your name on it actually worked? Unfortunately, the secret to getting rich is that there is no secret. Investors are constantly searching for the key that will unlock the market's many mysteries that will lead to the easy profits. This is why the bookshelves are full of books that promise to help you turn small amounts of money into millions of dollars overnight. *How to Make $30,000 in Just Seven Days. How I Turned $10,000 into $2 Million in Under a Year.*

   Don't believe anyone who tells people that getting rich very quickly is easy. Anyone who has done this had a healthy dose of luck involved. A person claiming to have the secret formula for easy wealth is probably a huckster or a charlatan. Building wealth requires patience and discipline. And if someone has the secret to getting rich quick, why would they reveal their secrets to you? Putting yourself out there as the high priest of getting rich is a great way to get people to believe in you, because people *want* to believe it exists. People will believe those who have confidence and speak with an air of certainty. "Here's where you should put your money right now," sounds much more reassuring than "Diversify your portfolio because no one knows what's going to happen in the future."

One of the consequences of the search for a winning lottery ticket in the markets is that it can lead investors to overpay for certain stocks, sectors, or asset classes at the worst possible times. When we think we've figured out the sure path to riches we tend to project the current trend into the future forever, reality be damned. There is no easy route to building wealth. It takes time, patience, discipline, and hard work. It can be simple, but it's definitely never going to be easy. Be very skeptical of anyone trying to sell you the dream of an easy road to riches.

2. **Not having a plan in place.**

There's really no way to guarantee with 100 percent certainty that your investment portfolio—filled with stocks, bonds, real estate, or any other asset—will be as successful as you would like it to be. But there is a sure way to fail—never implement a plan in the first place. It seems so trivial and basic to have an investment plan, much like creating a monthly budget for spending purposes. But it's going to be impossible to react with equanimity during all market conditions if you don't have a written plan in place to guide your actions. Investors without a plan are the ones who will surely fail on a consistent basis because they're constantly relying on their gut instincts to tell them what to do. Since successful investing is counterintuitive, this leads people to make the wrong moves at the wrong times. A plan is how you place constraints on your lesser self and ensure higher-probability decisions. An investor without a plan is no investor at all—they are a speculator.

3. Going with the herd instead of thinking for yourself.

Following the herd is what caused investors to pile into technology stocks in the late 1990s before the NASDAQ fell over 80 percent in value. It's what caused people to buy houses they couldn't afford in the mid-2000s during the real estate bubble. It's what caused the real estate market in the city of Tokyo to be worth four times as much as the entire real estate market in the United States in the late 1980s. Herding has caused every one of the greatest bubbles of all-time. This goes back to the Dutch tulip bubble in the 1600s that saw the price of a single tulip bulb sell for the equivalent of 10 years' wages for the average worker.[3]

Time and again people fall for the narrative that this time is different and things can go up in value forever. According to psychologists there are eight symptoms of groupthink that people need to be aware of (see Figure 2.1). Understanding these symptoms and acknowledging that they exist is the first step to minimizing their effects on your decision-making process.[4] It feels much safer to follow the crowd in the markets, and at times the crowd is right, but this can become dangerous at the extremes.

---

1. **An illusion of invulnerability:** Members ignore danger, take extreme risks, and are overly optimistic.
2. **Collective rationalization:** Members discredit and explain away warnings contrary to group thinking.
3. **Belief in inherent morality:** Members believe their decisions are morally correct, ignoring the ethical consequences of their decisions.
4. **Excessive stereotyping:** The group constructs negative stereotypes of rivals outside the group.
5. **Direct pressure on dissenters:** Members pressure any in the group who expresses arguments against the group's stereotypes, illusions, or commitments, viewing such opposition as disloyalty.
6. **Self-censorship:** Members withhold their dissenting views and counterarguments.
7. **Illusion of unanimity:** Members perceive falsely that everyone agrees with the group's decision; silence is seen as consent.
8. **Mind guards are appointed:** Some members appoint themselves to the role of protecting the group from adverse information that might threaten the group's complacency.

Figure 2.1   Eight Symptoms of Groupthink

4. **Focusing exclusively on the short term.**

With the 24-hour news cycle, every week there will be a new crisis that will pop up and grab investor's attention. Financial advisor and author Nick Murray summed this up best when he said, "There is virtually always an apocalypse du jour going on somewhere in the world. And on the rare occasions when there is not, journalism will simply invent one, and present it 24/7 as the incipient end of the world." As investors these events are difficult to deal with. The majority of the time they blow over or are a minor blip on the long-term market graph. Other times they can lead to painful losses. Sometimes short-term events matter to the markets and other times they don't. Investors have to concern themselves not with whether some event will affect the markets, but how it will affect their personal situation.

Trying to guess the outcome of every geopolitical event each week is a flip of the coin, at best. Focusing primarily on short-term outcomes is silly because they're completely out of your control. It's like the news organizations that try to explain why the market was up or down on a daily basis. No one really knows, but it makes us feel better if we can attach a narrative to those daily moves. Focusing on the short term only increases your activity and runs up huge trading and market impact costs from poorly timed decisions. You'll end up over-reacting every time the market rises or falls. Living and dying by every minor tick in the market is an unwarranted stress to add to your life. Plus, no one can guess which direction the markets will go over the short term anyways.

5. **Focusing only on those areas that are completely out of your control.**

The short-term moves in the market aren't the only things that are completely out of your control as an investor. There is a laundry list of complaints investors spit out on a daily basis—inflation, the actions of the president, Congress, the Federal Reserve, the economy, tax policy, the actions of either political party, the level of interest rates—the list could go on forever. These things all have something in common—you have no control over them whatsoever. You can't pick up the phone and complain to the president because you don't like his economic policies.

Maybe it's cathartic to complain about these things, but it won't help improve your financial situation one iota. The things you do control have a much larger impact on your bottom line—how much money you save, instituting a comprehensive investment plan, setting a reasonable asset allocation mix, defining your tolerance for risk, keeping your costs and activity in check, taking advantage of tax-deferred retirement accounts and making level-headed decisions.

6. **Taking the markets personally.**

Once you start to take the market's movements personally you've already lost. The market is never out to get you. The Fed doesn't have your portfolio in mind when setting monetary policy. The market does't have a vendetta against you every time you lose money or miss out on an opportunity for profit. When you personalize the market's moves, you fall into the trap of trying to be right rather than trying to make money. When you take things personally, your first instinct will be to blame others for losses instead of owning up to your own mistakes or the simple fact that not every investment strategy is going to be a winner at all times. Trying to be correct all the time switches your mindset from process to outcomes, which only increases your stress level. Constantly worrying about outcomes that are completely out of your control, especially in the short term, is asking for trouble from Mr. Market.

It's bad enough that investors get dinged in their pocketbooks when they take losses. Don't compound the issue by letting your ego make things far worse. There are no style points when investing, so there's no reason to feed your ego. When you become preoccupied with the fact that you sold a stock too soon or didn't buy early enough it's easy to look for someone to blame. But once you try to assign blame to anyone other than yourself or the random nature of the markets at time, you're allowing emotions to take over, which is when mistakes occur. We have to invest in the markets as they are, not as we wish them to be. When something goes wrong in either the markets or our own portfolios, the problem is not the markets. It's each of us individually. It's our perceptions, and how our reactions are affected by those perceptions. Learning how to lose money is actually much more important than learning how to make money in the markets because losing is inevitable. Investing is not as much about your actions as it is about your reactions and how they affect your thought process.

7. **Not admitting your limitations.**

Overconfidence is one of the biggest destroyers of wealth on the planet. It causes investors to assume their predictions about the future will be precise. It leads people to believe that they don't need to practice risk management. And it makes others believe that they have complete control over the markets. One of the most important theories to understand in the portfolio management process is Benjamin Graham's concept of the margin of safety. A margin of safety provides room for error in your judgment. It's acknowledgment that you can't always be right all the time. A margin of safety takes into account a wide range of possibilities so the investor isn't left broke and penniless from making an investment with a 100 percent degree of certainty It provides a cushion for our inability to predict the future.

Investors who are unwilling to admit their limitations don't provide themselves a margin of safety. They assume they will be right at all times. They never admit when they're wrong, but choose to find fault in their model or the market. One of the easiest ways to give yourself a margin of safety is to practice diversification. Spreading your money across a wide range of investments, asset classes, and geographies is the ultimate form of saying, "I have no idea what's going to happen in the future." Intelligent investors plan on a wide range of outcomes to shield themselves from crushing losses through risk management and humility.

The Biggest Problem of All

Don't just take my word for it on the poor behavior of investors. Professors Brad Barber and Terrance Odean of the University of California have been studying investor behavior and compiling data on the collective mistakes of investors for a number of years now. For instance, investors trade too much and this activity hurts performance from mistimed buys and sells and increased costs. Investors are overconfident and prefer lottery ticket stocks because we are thrill seekers who love to chase the action in the most speculative investments. When buying individual stocks, people tend to invest only in those companies they're familiar with. They sell winners and hold losers, because of an anchoring to past prices. Instead of judging an investment by its current value, investors think in terms of the original price they paid and hope that it will someday get back to their cost value before they sell. We repeat past behaviors that coincide with pleasure and avoid those that caused pain, which leads investors to seek short-term comfort over long-term gains. Finally, investors fail to diversify, one of the easiest risks of all to minimize.[5]

Through all of the negative knowledge I've shared here there is one unifying theme that causes investors, both large and small, to make mistakes with their money on a consistent basis—it's because we're human. The thing that sets us apart from other mammals is our emotions. Emotions are not all bad. You just have to determine when they are useful and when they are destructive to be able to control them in certain situations.

There are many areas in your life that call for emotional reactions—you should get emotional on your wedding day or during the birth of your child. But emotions are the enemy of good investment decisions. Let me repeat that one more time for effect: emotions are the enemy of good investment decisions.

All of the mistakes I've listed boil down to human nature and our inherent cognitive biases. Emotions force investors to confuse their time horizon with everyone else's, which causes a misalignment of goals as people ignore their personal circumstances. As the markets move up and down, so, too, do people's tolerance for risk. It feels better to be buying *after* stocks have risen a great deal, just like it feels better to be selling stocks *after* they have gotten crushed. Another issue facing investors is that they would like an all-clear signal that lets them know exactly when to buy stocks. Others are always waiting until "things get better." Emotions lead to more activity than is necessary, as investors jump from investment strategy to investment strategy in hopes of timing everything perfectly. Investors worry only about what could go right with an investment and ignore what could go wrong. They obsess over the daily moves in the market even though they have decades until retirement.

We are constantly fighting the last war by letting the recency effect lead us to make decisions based on what we wish we had done in last cycle. The endowment effect causes investors to overvalue investments that they already own. The confirmation bias draws us into only those sources that agree with our current mindset instead of looking for opposing viewpoints. An availability bias means whatever is in front of us right now is what we'll base our decisions simply because it's there.

Investing isn't only about understanding market history, portfolio construction, mutual funds, and ETFs. None of that matters if we don't understand how our natural human inclinations and cognitive biases can wreak havoc on our decision-making process. You also have to understand the psychology of others, because even if you behave, you must understand that the market can go bonkers from time to time, whether you participate in the madness of the crowd or not. Fear, greed, euphoria, panic, speculation, envy—these are the killers of your portfolio

Even if you've never made any of these mistakes in the past, figuring out where others consistently go wrong is one of the best ways to ensure your own success. There are many ways to make money, but when it really comes down to it, the easiest way to lose money is because of psychological and behavioral issues. Now that you have a crash course in negative knowledge, let's look at the flip side of the coin to see what traits define a successful investor.

Traits of a Successful Investor

Now that you know what not to do, here are six traits that all successful investors share.

1. **Emotional intelligence.**

    Investors need a certain level of intelligence to succeed in the markets. But having the highest IQ in the room isn't the most important thing. Having the correct temperament is far more important than intellect over time. There are plenty of intelligent people who make extremely irrational decisions when dealing with their finances. You don't have to ace your SATs to be able to succeed in the financial markets. Intelligence is no substitute for wisdom. Wise people try to learn from their mistakes and the mistakes of others.

    Psychologist Daniel Goleman literally wrote the book—called *Emotional Intelligence*—on this subject. Goleman says emotional intelligence is "the capacity for recognizing our own feelings and those of others, for motivating ourselves, and for managing emotions well in ourselves and in our relationships." In the book, Goleman describes five basic competencies for emotional intelligence: (1) self-awareness, (2) self-regulation, (3) motivation, (4) empathy, and (5) social skills.

Self-awareness is the ability to understand how emotions affect yourself and other people. Self-awareness is how investors can extinguish overconfidence from ever finding its way into their investment process. You must be willing to identify your current emotional state to be self-aware, so self-reflection is the key here. Self-regulation is the ability to control impulsive decisions. The best way to account for a deficiency in this area is to create a plan that accounts for a lack of self-regulation. As we'll see later in the book, self-control isn't something people can do all the time without becoming fatigued. Motivation is having a passion for what you do along with a curiosity for learning. Once you start to learn about how the world operates, you realize the more you learn, the less you really know and understand. Learning is a continuous process for intelligent investors. Empathy is the ability to understand the emotional make-up of others. It's not enough to understand your own psychological tendencies. You also have to comprehend how the psychology of the herd works. It doesn't matter how rational you are in your approach; if you don't appreciate how silly the market can get from time to time, you'll eventually crack.

2. Patience.

There's no reason to be in a hurry to get wealthy. In 2014, it was estimated that Warren Buffett's net worth was close to $60 billion. When he was approaching 60 years old in 1989, his net worth was "only" $3.8 billion. So almost 95 percent of Buffett's wealth has been created after the age of 60 (and probably more than that since he's given away some of his stock to charity). This speaks to the power of compound interest. As Buffett once said, "Charlie [Munger] and I always knew we would become very wealthy, but we weren't in a hurry. Even if you're a slightly above average investor who spends less than you earn, over a lifetime you cannot help but get very wealthy—if you're patient."[6] Compound interest doesn't

Emily DiDonato

Photographer: Kayt Jones • Location: Namibia

Friday
14

March 2014

S	M	T	W	T	F
2	3	4	5	6	7
9	10	11	12	13	14
16	17	18	19	20	21
23	24	25	26	27	28
30	31				

happen overnight. It takes time and slowly builds on itself until it becomes a machine.

3. **Calm during times of chaos.**

   With a little over three minutes to play in Super Bowl XXIII, the San Francisco 49ers were down by three points to the Cincinnati Bengals. As they entered the huddle for the possible game-winning drive, 49ers quarterback Joe Montana surveyed the stadium and said to his teammate, Harris Barton, "There, in the stands, standing near the exit ramp. Isn't that John Candy?" The 49ers then proceeded to march down the field 92 yards to score with a game-winning touchdown pass from Montana to John Taylor. It was said Montana has a mythical calmness about him during times of chaos. He was never the most athletic and didn't have the strongest arm in the NFL, but he was cool under pressure. It's one of the reasons he won four Super Bowls. There he was during the most important drive of his life, pointing out an actor in the stands to calm not only himself, but his teammates, as well.[7] This is how the best investors react during a market crash or economic crisis. They don't get rattled. They remain calm and follow their process. When everyone else is panicking, successful investors are at their best.

4. **The ability to say "I don't know."**

   When asked what it is in his career that he had to un-learn to become a better investor, legendary author and investor Peter Bernstein replied, "That I knew what the future held, I guess. That you can figure this thing out. I mean, I've become increasingly humble about it over time and comfortable with that. You have to understand that being wrong is part of the process. And I try to shut up at cocktail parties. You have to keep learning that you don't know, because you find models that work, ways to make money, and then they blow sky-high. There's always somebody around who looks smart."[8]

   The ability to stay within your circle of competence and understand that which you don't know is paramount to your success as an investor. You don't need to have an opinion on everything. There's no reason to try to invest in every fad investment fund or trend that's developing. The truly great investors stick to their knitting and stay away from that which they don't understand or those areas in which they don't have an edge. When you try to be all things at all times as an investor you end up losing touch with reality because you don't focus on the important aspects of portfolio management.

Daniel Kahneman once said, "Two important facts about our minds: We can be blind to the obvious and also blind to the blindness." Psychologists find that people are aware of the biased thinking in others, but they tend to underestimate biased thinking in themselves. A study of medical residents founds that 61 percent said they were not influenced by gifts from the drug companies, but only 16 percent said the same thing about other physicians.[9] Everyone else is an idiot, but surely not me, is a dangerous attitude to carry. Admitting the fact that you don't know everything is a good first step towards becoming a better investor and understanding your own biased behavior.

5. **Understand history.**

Without a firm grasp of history investors are doomed to repeat past mistakes. The cycle of manias and panics repeats itself throughout history because human nature remains. From the South Sea Bubble to the Great Recession and everything in between if there's one constant across time in all markets it's the fact that human nature eventually causes the pendulum to swing too far in either direction, leading to the boom-and-bust cycle. Investors forget their history and simply extrapolate the most recent market cycle forever into the future at their own peril.

Looking back at historical market performance data is also a key to understanding the present. Even if we don't know exactly what to do going forward, looking back at history is a good way to figure out what not to do so you don't repeat past mistakes. Past performance has absolutely no bearing on future performance, but this doesn't mean that we discard historical results altogether just because they can't be used to make perfect market forecasts. Although the future will always be different than the past, you can still use history to guide your actions from a probabilistic standpoint. The history of stock and bond returns tells us nothing about the precise future returns of either asset class, but they are useful as a measure of risk. We know that the stock market can drop

50 to 80 percent in a market crash, and it can rise by the same amount just as fast.

Understanding what can happen and what usually happens can help investors set the proper risk controls on themselves and their portfolio. Historical numbers will never be perfect, but what other choice do we have as investors? As Warren Buffett has famously said, "I would rather be approximately right than precisely wrong." A historical view can—or should—also be comforting when things get really bad during a recession or a market crash. The basic behavior of participants in the financial markets is little changed over time, so learning as much about market history as possible is one of the best ways to develop the correct mindset to keep your behavior in check.

6. **Discipline.**

It doesn't matter how great an investment strategy one has if they are unable to drum up the requisite discipline to follow it over various market cycles. Even the most mediocre of portfolios that is dutifully followed will perform better than the most optimized portfolio that is not. Famed quant hedge fund manager Cliff Asness summed this up nicely when he said, "The great strategy you can't stick with is obviously vastly inferior to the very good strategy you can stick with." Those who are able to calmly stay the course and follow their process when everyone else around them is losing their heads will be the investors that succeed at the expense of others. One of the worst parts about the financial markets is that not everyone can win. In a very broad sense, someone must fail for you to succeed since there is always a buyer and a seller of every security. Discipline is the ultimate decider between the winners and the losers in the financial markets.

We like to think we all make rational decisions based on our choices and that it's a level playing field, but the truth is some people were simply born with different wiring which allows them to have more success. There are five factors that affect our personalities: extraversion, openness, agreeableness, neuroticism, and conscientiousness. The last one, conscientiousness, is closely related to self-control and discipline. Studies find that conscientious-minded people tend to save more money because they don't make impulse purchases or spend too much money on things they don't need. In fact, those who exhibit this trait tend to accumulate more wealth than less conscientious people, even after accounting for things like education, income, and cognitive abilities.[10]

If you're one of the lucky conscientious people, good for you. Take advantage of your self-control and don't waste it. Even then, overconfidence can become an issue, so always stay humble or the market will do it for you. But if you're not blessed with these types of attributes, don't despair. It doesn't mean you give up. You just have to create systems to automate conscientious behavior. No one is born with every single trait of a successful investor and none of the flaws. The good news is that you don't have to be born conscientious to make conscientious decisions on a regular basis. Even the brightest people have their flaws. The ones that succeed are those who are adept at systematically negating those flaws by creating processes to weed out bad behavior and glaring weaknesses.

Unfortunately, intelligence and self-control alone are not enough to change bad behavior. There was a study performed in Africa about how the knowledge of preventive measures for the spread of HIV/AIDS would change the resulting sexual behavior in people with that knowledge. In Botswana, over 90 percent of the men in the study said they understood that using a condom would help prevent the spread of this deadly disease, but only 70 percent of them admitted to using a condom. For woman it was actually far worse. There were 92 percent that said they knew condoms prevented HIV/AIDS, but only 63 percent reported the use of a condom.[11] Information alone will not help change your behavior, even with dire consequences. You have to systematically root out bad behavior by automating good decisions to stay out of your own way.

Psychologists have found the following five conditions can lead to bad behavior and poor decision making:

1. When the problem is complex.
2. When there's incomplete information and the information changes.
3. When goals change or compete with one another.
4. When there is high stress or high stakes involved.
5. When we interact with others to make decisions.[12]

Sound familiar? This basically is a description of the circumstances people face every time they are forced to make a financial decision. In the next section, we'll see if two of the greatest investors of all-time can help make it easier for investors to make good decisions, even though they face difficult circumstances.

Standing on the Shoulders of Giants

Hang out with people better than you and you cannot help but improve.
—Warren Buffett

One of the best ways to learn how to make better decisions is by studying the greats in your field of choice. Much of this learning for me, outside of my experience with the markets, has come through good, old-fashioned books. The very first investment book I ever read was *The Intelligent Investor* by Benjamin Graham. Graham was Warren Buffett's mentor and is known as the father of value investing. His analogy of the stock market as an accommodating fellow named Mr. Market has stuck with me ever since. I always assumed that the stock market was controlled by the smartest, most intelligent investors in the world. But that intelligence doesn't mean a thing when emotions take over. Some days Mr. Market feels depressed and offers lower prices in the markets. Other days he feels euphoric and offers higher prices. But you can feel free to ignore his volatile mood swings because he will always come back again the next day. How you choose to act under these conditions is up to you.

I was instantly hooked on the stock market and the process of investing after reading Graham. But I didn't take away the correct lessons from the *Intelligent Investor* right away. It took some time. Initially, with my youthful confidence, I decided I would try to become the next Warren Buffett. I read everything I could find on Buffett and then moved on to Peter Lynch, George Soros, Seth Klarman, Howard Marks, Charlie Munger, and many of the other greats. I was planning on knocking it out of the park like these sages had done. Little did I realize this was not the path to take to become a successful investor.

It took me many mistakes and lessons learned, but I finally came to a realization—I am not Warren Buffett nor will I ever become the Oracle of Omaha. It's like saying I want to be the Michael Jordan of investing. Is that a realistic goal? Of course not, but unlike the NBA—where you're never going to be able to find yourself on the same court as the best basketball players in the world—everyone invests on the same playing field in the financial markets. Anyone can open a brokerage account and trade the same stocks and bonds that the professionals are buying and selling (up to a point).

I paid my tuition to the market and experienced some losses, but it was worth it because I came to the realization that I didn't need to become an extraordinary investor to be successful. And by trying to become an extraordinary investor it only made things worse. The harder you try to become the world's best investor, the easier it is to become one of the worst.

This doesn't mean you can't learn many lessons from the world's greatest investors, though. Far from it. Most people that track the greats just seek the wrong lessons. Everyone wants to read the lists that show the *Top 10 Stocks Warren Buffett Might Be Buying Today.*

The whole point of this book is that top 10 lists and tactics are not going to help you build or preserve wealth. They are short-term fixes and, more often than not, useless in the grand scheme of things. I can't offer you a guaranteed recipe for success in five easy steps. But no one else can either. The reason get rich quick books sell is because we all hold out hope that it's possible. Sure, some people can get lucky, for a while. But eventually that luck runs out without the discipline, patience, and process in place to make it stick.

These are the true lessons that I learned in my studies of the world's greatest investors. It's unrealistic to assume you will have the same objectives and opportunities that a billionaire will have. But the most important lessons have nothing to do with specific investments and everything to do with making good decisions and developing the correct temperament. With that in mind, here are my three biggest takeaways from two of the greatest investors of all-time: Buffett and his partner at Berkshire Hathaway, Charlie Munger.

1. Simplify.

Charlie Munger, Warren Buffett's right-hand man at Berkshire Hathaway, is something of a modern-day Benjamin Franklin. Not in the sense that Franklin was famous for many of his inventions, but in the way that he thinks about the world around him and how he makes decisions. Franklin was successful in a number of endeavors and used a wide variety of disciplines to formulate his thoughts and theories. Munger is famous for his elementary, worldly wisdom that draws upon a number of different fields to make better decisions. Munger's latticework of mental models approach includes biology, philosophy, psychology, math, economics, engineering and many more subjects. He even has a book that's crafted after Franklin's pseudonymous *Poor Richard's Almanack* called *Poor Charlie's Almanack*.

The interesting thing about very intelligent and successful people is that they're usually the ones who have figured out that making things simple is the correct path to success. Because they understand how things work, they are able to appreciate and utilize simplicity. Those who don't have a hard time grasping this. Munger says figuring out the no-brainers is the first step. He writes, "My first helpful notion is that it is usually best to simplify problems by deciding big 'no-brainer' questions first." This seems obvious, but it's difficult for people to see the beauty in simplicity when everyone else is in search of complexity. Munger continues, "The simple idea may appear too obvious to be useful, but there is an old two-part rule that often works wonders in business, science and elsewhere: (1) take a simple, basic idea and (2) take it very seriously."

Albert Einstein, the man considered by many to be one of the smartest people to ever live, also practiced simplicity to solve problems. Instead of looking at very specific data to try to solve problems, Einstein would look for very broad, overarching, and simple principles that could be applied with other big-picture theories to create truly ground-breaking work. Einstein always said that a principle by itself predicts nothing specific, but once you combined a number of principles together there could be unlimited implications on the problems you could solve.[13]

Occam's razor states that complicated assumptions may work out, but in an uncertain world, the simpler the choice, the better. Just like with David Swensen, sometimes it takes a very intelligent person to see and experience complexity before they come to the realization that simplicity works better. Munger understands this as well as anyone.

Buffett echoes Munger's claims by showing how reducing the number of decisions they have to make has improved their results over time.

> Charlie and I decided long ago that in an investment lifetime it's just too hard to make hundreds of smart decisions. That judgment became ever more compelling as Berkshire's capital mushroomed and the universe of investments that could significantly affect our results shrank dramatically. Therefore, we adopted a strategy that required our being smart—and not too smart at that—only a very few times. Indeed, we'll now settle for one good idea a year. (Charlie says it's my turn.)
>
> Over the [past] 35 years, American business has delivered terrific results. It should therefore have been easy for investors to earn juicy returns: All they had to do was piggyback Corporate America in a diversified, low-expense way. An index fund that they never touched would have done the job. Instead many investors have had experiences ranging from mediocre to disastrous.[14]

Every investor should be able to explain their investment philosophy in a 60-second elevator pitch. If you cannot do this, either your strategy is far too complex or you don't really have a philosophy to begin with (more on this in Chapter 5). On this matter, Buffett says, "Our investments continue to be few in number and simple in concept: The truly big investment idea can usually be explained in a short paragraph."

2. **Invert to solve problems.**
   In the same vein as the negative knowledge section from earlier in the chapter, Munger learned to turn problems upside down or to look at them backwards. His famous saying is, "Invert, always invert." Looking at things from this point of view can help investors realize where it is they are going wrong instead of always trying to figure out how to make things perfect. Munger says, "It is not enough to think problems through forward. You must also think in reverse, much like the rustic who wanted to know where he was going to die so that he'd never go there. Indeed, many problems can't be solved forward."

Buffett's take is similar in that he thinks it's more important to reduce unforced errors than it is to get everything perfect: "What counts for most people in investing is not how much they know, but rather how realistically they define what they don't know. An investor needs to do very few things right as long as he or she avoids big mistakes."

3. **Stay open-minded.**

Munger doesn't believe in having a narrow focus on just one area of expertise. The big breakthroughs can only come from thinking in terms of a number of different disciplines. He says as much, "Really big effects, lollapalooza effects, will often come only from large combinations of factors. For instance, tuberculosis was tamed, at least for a long time, only by routine combined use in each case of three different drugs. And other lollapalooza effects, like the flight of an airplane, follow a similar pattern."[15]

The lollapalooza effects that Munger describes can also work against the market when emotions are taken to the extreme. This is why Buffett says it's better to err on the side of caution when making predictions about where the market is heading. He says, "We have no idea—and never have had—whether the market is going to go up, down, or sideways in the near- or intermediate-term future. What we do know, however, is that occasional outbreaks of those two super-contagious diseases, fear and greed, will forever occur in the investment community. The timing of these epidemics will be unpredictable. And the market aberrations produced by them will be equally unpredictable, both as to duration and degree."

Simplify, invert, and broaden your horizons and things can become much easier when making decisions. The advantages are many says Munger, "There are huge advantages for an individual to get into position where you make a few great investments and just sit back. You're paying less to brokers. You're listening to less nonsense. ... If it works, the governmental tax system gives you an extra one, two, or three percentage points per annum with compound effects."

Getting rid of the nonsense is easier said than done. It's not that people don't have the right intentions. Everyone wants to do the right thing. It's just that we humans lack the requisite willpower necessary to make lasting changes in our behavioral patterns. The best investment strategy is the one that you can follow. The worst investment strategy is the one that cannot be followed. It's not so much about getting things exactly right ... it's about not getting things completely wrong.

Key Takeaways from Chapter 2

- Most people will get much more out of destroying their own wrong ideas than trying to come up with new ones all the time. Once you get rid of the clutter, all that's left will be the good stuff that you can use to improve your results.
- There are many lessons you can learn from some of the greatest investors of all-time—patience, simplicity, discipline— but that doesn't mean you can expect to invest just like your favorite billionaire. Understand your own limitations and never try to complicate the investment process.
- The most successful investors utilize different strategies within their portfolios but they all share the ability to control their emotions when everyone else around them is losing their cool. Emotional control is far more important than your SAT score.

Notes

1. Patrick Burns, "Betterment's Quest for Behavior Gap Zero," Betterment.com, www.betterment.com/resources/investment-strategy/behavioral-finance-investing-strategy/betterments-quest-behavior-gap-zero/.
2. Benjamin Loos, Steffan Meyer, Joachim Weber, and Andreas Hackenthal, "Which Investor Behaviors Really Matter for Individual Investors?" Social Science Research Network, December 2014, http://papers.ssrn.com/sol3/papers.cfm?abstract_id=2381435.
3. Edward Chancellor, *Devil Take the Hindmost* (New York: Plume, 2000).
4. Irvin Janis and Leon Man, *Decision Making: A Psychological Analysis of Conflict, Choice and Commitment"* (New York, Free Press, 1977).
5. Brad Barber and Terrance Odean, "The Behavior of Individual Investors," Haas School of Business, September 2011.
6. Guy Spier, *The Education of a Value Investor: My Transformative Quest for Wealth, Wisdom, and Enlightenment* (New York: Palgrave Macmillan, 2014).

7. Larry Schwartz, "Montana Was the Comeback King," ESPN.com, https://espn.go.com/sportscentury/features/00016306.html.
8. Jason Zweig, "Peter's Uncertainty Principle," *Money Magazine*, November 2004.
9. Dan Gardner, *The Science of Fear: How the Culture of Fear Manipulates Your Brain* (New York: Plume, 2009).
10. Mier Statman, "Mandatory Retirement Savings," Social Science Research Network, March 2013, http://papers.ssrn.com/sol3/papers.cfm?abstract_id=2230546.
11. James Montier, *The Little Book of Behavioral Investing: How Not to Be Your Own Worst Enemy* (Hoboken, NJ: John Wiley & Sons, 2010).
12. Gary Klein, *Sources of Power: How People Make Decisions* (Cambridge, MA: MIT Press, 1999).
13. David Hestenes, review of *Imagery in Scientific Thought*, by Arthur I. Miller, *New Ideas in Psychology* 8, no. 2 (1990), http://modeling.asu.edu/R&E/SecretsGenius.pdf.
14. Warren Buffett, Letter to Shareholders, 1993, www.berkshirehathaway.com/letters/1993.html.
15. Janet Lowe, *Damn Right: Behind the Scenes with Berkshire Hathaway Billionaire Charlie Munger* (Hoboken, NJ: John Wiley & Sons, 2003).

3

Defining Market and Portfolio Risk

The stock market is a giant distraction to the business of investing.
—John Bogle

In the 1960s there was a French film called *The Lovers (Les Amants)*. It turned out to be a little risqué for some people in the Midwest. The state of Ohio ruled the film to be obscene and pornographic. The case eventually made it all the way to the Supreme Court, where it was ruled that the movie was not, in fact, too obscene to be viewed by the public. Justice Potter Stewart had this to say when describing the film and pornography in general, "I shall not today attempt further to define the kinds of material I understand to be embraced within that shorthand description ['hard-core pornography'], and perhaps I could never succeed in intelligibly doing so. But I know it when I see it, and the motion picture involved in this case is not that."[1]

Most investors assume that risk is a form of "I know it when I see it." Unfortunately, risk is nearly impossible to define because it has so many permutations. To some it's volatility. To others it's losing money. Longevity risk—outliving your money—is probably the biggest risk of all. Then you have all of the risks within each investment class: duration, interest rates, earnings shortfalls, recessions, permanent impairment, innovation, competition, and so on. The list could seemingly go on forever.

If there is an ironclad rule in the world of investing, it's that risk and reward are always and forever attached at the hip. You can't expect to earn outsized gains if you don't expose yourself to the possibility of outsized losses. If you are seeking the safety of your principal, you have to be willing to give up on the prospect of higher returns. If you are seeking to compound your wealth through higher investment returns, you have to be willing to let go of the idea that your money won't fluctuate and possibly fall in the short to intermediate term. You have to seek a balance within your own portfolio, but understand that there is no such thing as a free lunch.

Here are the annual returns for stocks, bonds, and cash going back to 1928 (stocks are represented by the S&P 500; bonds by 10-year U.S. government-issued treasuries, and cash by three-month Treasury bills):[2]

Stocks 9.6 percent
Bonds 4.9 percent
Cash 3.5 percent

These are the nominal returns for each asset class. Since purchasing power isn't stable over the long term, investors have to think about the risk of inflation as well. If you take into account the effects of inflation, these are the real returns over the same time frame:

Stocks 6.5 percent
Bonds 1.9 percent
Cash 0.5 percent

It's obvious that stocks have been an investor's best bet for building wealth and growing their savings over the very long term. In the simplest terms possible, the reason that stocks earn higher returns than bonds or cash over time is because there will be periods of excruciating losses in stocks. Stocks have earned more than three times as much as bonds over time because the return stream can be so inconsistent from year to year. The average 9.6 percent annual return is anything but average over any given year, as you can see in Figure 3.1.

In Finance 101, one of the first lessons they teach you is that every investment's value today is based on the future cash flows it will produce in the future. In the case of stocks, the value is thus based on the future aggregate stream of dividends and earnings that they will produce. But no one really knows what these cash flows

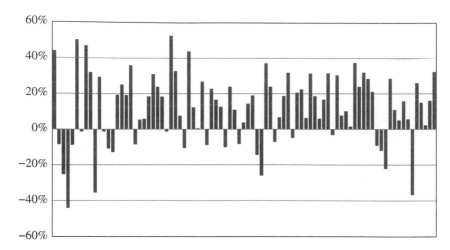

Figure 3.1   Annual Stock Market Returns, 1928–2013 (Standard & Poor's 500)
Source: Aswath Damodaran.

will be with any certainty. It's impossible to predict where human ingenuity will take us or what the future economic environment will look like. So stocks trade in the short to intermediate term based on emotions, not fundamentals. Trends and sentiment can overwhelm the underlying fundamentals in the short term. The reason markets exist and change so frequently is because of differences in opinions, goals, and time horizons. In many ways, the short-term movements in the stock market are really just one big psychological experiment on human nature, while in the longer-term, fundamentals tend to be the driving force.

Bonds are a different story. Bonds—debt instruments really— have contractually obligated cash flow payments. Think about a bond like taking out a mortgage on your house, but instead of being obligated to pay back the amount borrowed, investors are the borrowers. And those taking out a mortgage are corporations, governments, and municipalities. If you stop making mortgage payments, you default on the loan and the bank takes your house since it's used as collateral. If you are a credit-worthy borrower you pay a lower interest rate. If you have terrible credit or have been bankrupt in the past your interest rate will be much higher. Generally, this is how bonds work and it's why they are considered to be safer than stocks. Safer, in this sense, means that it's more likely that your investment will

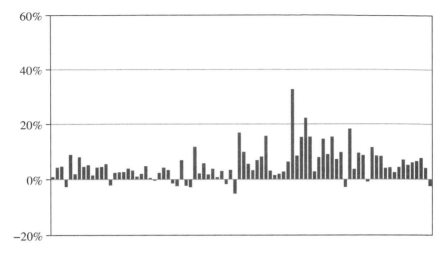

Figure 3.2   Annual Bond Returns, 1928–2013 (10-Year Treasury Bonds)
Source: Aswath Damodaran.

pay you back in a reasonable period of time. Corporations are under no contractual agreement to pay back their stock shareholders with cash flows for dividends or earnings. But they are contractually obligated to pay back bondholders. Otherwise, like the bank taking your house, the assets of the firm could be sold off in bankruptcy and the bond holders would be paid out accordingly based on the value of the assets.

Hence, stocks have a risk premium over bonds. There's more uncertainty in the outcome of the stock market than there is the bond market over the short-term. Stocks have a higher return on capital and more volatility in their results. You can see in Figure 3.2 that bonds fluctuate in value much less than stocks because of the underlying cash flows and the way that they are structured.

There's no way you can avoid risk in the financial markets if you hope to beat inflation over the long term and earn a respectable return on your portfolio. Stocks have outperformed bonds over the majority of longer-term cycles, but bonds provide stability when you need it the most. Stocks wouldn't offer a risk premium over bonds if they didn't have these periodic large selloffs.

Because the debt markets are vitally important to a functioning global economy, the bond market is actually larger than the stock

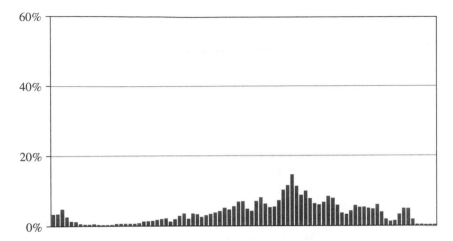

Figure 3.3   Annual Cash Returns, 1928–2013 (Three-Month Treasury Bills)
Source: Aswath Damodaran.

market. Bond investors generally worry about when they're going to get paid back and how they're going to get paid back. But this amount is capped by the interest rate on the bond and the maturity date of the bond. Stock investors generally worry about how much money they're going to make in price appreciation and dividends. My first boss in the industry told me stocks are what you invest in to get rich and bonds are what you invest in to stay rich. But you can see from the annual return chart that even bonds can periodically lose money, even if it's not close to the same magnitude as the drops in stock prices.

For those investors who don't want any chance of a decline in principal value, cash or T-bills are the safest form of short-term protection. You can see in Figure 3.3 that cash never loses any value in nominal terms, but for this protection from principal loss, investors are paid less over time. This is how risk and reward are supposed to work. It's never going to be easy, unfortunately. Parking your hard-earned savings in a money market or savings account isn't going to earn you much in the way of compound interest. At best you should hope to keep up with inflation. This is why an understanding of your time horizon is so utterly important. If you need to spend the money within five years or less, think long and hard about putting that money to work in the stock market. The short-term risks usually exceed the possible rewards over that short of a time frame.

If you have an intermediate goal, high-quality bonds are a good alternative, but even they can fall in value at times. If you have to spend your money tomorrow or within the next year, safety of principal is probably much more important than how much interest income you earn on your cash. One of the best forms of risk management is having enough liquid assets on hand so you aren't forced to sell your risk assets (read: stocks) during market crashes or corrections.

Looking at the performance chart of cash over time makes some investors feel much more comfortable playing it safe. There are no losses on this chart. The annual returns are fairly stable over time. The problem is that to get that safety of principle you have to give up any hope of higher long-term returns. To put the cash returns in context, the 0.5 percent annual return after inflation would mean that it would take an investor almost 150 years to double their investment. With the 6.5 percent historical real return in the stock market, it would take roughly 11 years to double your money.

The first thing that should jump out at you when looking at the charts for stocks, bonds, and cash is the variability in the performance numbers. The best annual return for stocks was 52.6 percent while the largest annual loss was –43.8 percent, a range in returns of almost 97 percent. For bonds, the best return was 32.8 percent while the lowest was –11.1 percent, for a range of nearly 44 percent. And for T-bills the difference between high and low was around 14 percent. Think about these numbers this way—one of the reasons stocks are able to earn higher returns for investors over time is because there are periods where you are able to buy at much lower levels to boost your performance. Not many investors have the requisite intestinal fortitude to pull this off, which is why some investors succeed while others fail. Some investors get scared out of stocks at the worst possible time and that wealth is transferred from the proverbial weak hands to the strong hands.

This doesn't mean you are guaranteed to earn the average return simply because you hold your stocks for longer periods. See Table 3.1 to see that each decade is unique and there are 10-year long periods—sometimes longer—where bonds outperform stocks. But the longer the holding period for the stock market as a whole, the better your odds of earning a positive return. It doesn't mean stocks

Table 3.1   Annual Returns by Decade

	Stocks	Bonds
1930s	−0.9%	4.0%
1940s	8.5%	2.5%
1950s	19.5%	0.8%
1960s	7.7%	2.4%
1970s	5.9%	5.4%
1980s	17.3%	12.0%
1990s	18.1%	7.4%
2000s	−1.0%	6.3%
2010s	15.7%	4.2%

Source: Aswath Damodaran.

are any less risky over longer time frames, because if you pick a terrible end point, say the depths of the market crash in early 2009, even a longer-term performance number might not look so great. But by increasing your holding period you increase your likelihood of success, and diversifying across time through the process of dollar cost averaging into stocks also helps your odds because you aren't reliant on any one period or lump sum to do the heavy lifting for you.

You also have to remember that these long-term performance numbers for stocks don't include any fees, taxes, or transaction costs. They're simple historical performance numbers. But they also aren't 9.6 percent per year because someone traded in and out of them when they felt like it. They aren't 9.6 percent because an investor side-stepped the latest market crash. They are 9.6 percent including the really good times and the really bad times—wars, recessions, bubbles, crashes, and everything in-between. Nothing is guaranteed, but your probability is greatly improved with a longer time horizon, no matter what happens in the interim.

The long-term trend in stocks has been up, but it has never been easy. There have been twenty separate periods of at least a 20 percent decline or more since 1928. Only about 6 percent of the time does the market finish the calendar year within the range of 7 to 12 percent annual returns. Over 35 percent of the time it's up more than 20 percent and more than 22 percent of the time it's down 5 percent or more. Some call this volatility but, really it's just variation around the average. This variation is what helps some by offering opportunities to profit, yet hurts others by offering opportunities to buy on greed and sell on fear.

Volatility: Risk or Opportunity?

Variation around the average is one of the most widely used risk metrics in the world of finance. Some call it volatility while others prefer the statistical definition of standard deviation. It sounds fancy, but standard deviation is simply the variation of results around an average. The higher the standard deviation, the further away from the average the prices tend to move. If you have a standard deviation of 20 percent that means that most of the time you can expect the returns to fall somewhere between plus or minus 20 percent of the average. So if the average performance of a certain investment is 10 percent a year you could reasonably expect the returns to fall somewhere between −10 and 30 percent, most of the time. And that "most of the time" matters a great deal because there are always going to be outlier events that fall outside of the normal distribution of returns. Statistics are clean, but the real world is messy.

Stock returns are much more variable than bond returns so they have a higher standard deviation. This is obvious when looking at the charts, but it's less obvious whether or not this is really the right way to measure risk for investors. The reason the finance industry has latched on to volatility as a proxy for risk is because it's easy to measure. If something can be measured, it can be communicated. If something can be communicated, it can be built into a narrative. And once a narrative takes off it can be framed almost any way a person wants to take it. I'm not trying to say that volatility isn't a risk, but it's certainly not the biggest risk for those investors that understand how it works.

For someone who needs to spend their cash tomorrow, variation is a huge risk. But for someone who has many decades to invest their savings, variation can be looked at as an opportunity when volatility strikes. Thus, context matters when determining risk in the markets. Price declines in the stock market actually improve long-term returns by offering lower prices and higher dividend yields. Therefore, risk should not be defined as volatility, but how you react to that volatility. The biggest risk for most investors comes from making poor decisions during bad times. The first step is to acknowledge that volatility is a fact of life in risky assets. This will help you design your investment plan to account for the inevitable fluctuations, in both the markets and your emotions.

Understanding Rule Number 1 of Investing

Warren Buffett has famously stated two simple rules for investing, "Rule Number 1: Never lose money. Rule Number 2: Never forget rule number one." If you look at the historical performance of Buffett's holding company, Berkshire Hathaway, in Table 3.2, we have an apparent contradiction to these rules. Buffett has seen the value of his stock in Berkshire get absolutely destroyed over the years a number of times. In fact, since 1980 alone the stock has fallen more than 30 percent on four separate occasions:

Those are outright crashes in Buffett's stock price. Is this a case of amateur hour from the Oracle of Omaha? Is Buffett not following his own rules? No, because, as always, context matters here. How much did Buffett actually lose during these four separate crashes? The answer may surprise you—technically he lost $0. Nothing, nada, zilch. How can this be? Because he never sold a single share of Berkshire Hathaway during these downturns. He never got scared out of his position and he wasn't forced to sell for liquidity or spending reasons. On paper, Buffett was down hundreds of millions or even billions of dollars, but he never locked in those losses by selling. Risk really only matters if it has consequences attached to it, either through a liquidity event because you're forced to sell or psychologically because you make a huge mistake at the wrong time.

In this sense, true risk is that which is irreversible. Volatility is temporary but if you lock in losses by selling after a crash has occurred, you now put yourself at risk of missing out on future gains at the worst possible time. This is especially true if you never have the guts to get back in. Most investors spend their time worrying about their risk profile on a daily, weekly, monthly, or even annual basis. If you're

Table 3.2   Buffett's Stock Losses

Time Frame	BRK-A Losses
1987	−37%
1989–1990	−37%
1998–2000	−49%
2007–2009	−51%

Source: Yahoo! Finance.

able to change your mindset from these shorter time frames to thinking in terms of five years or even a decade as your definition of short term then it completely changes your outlook, investment performance, and probability for success. It also ensures you won't mess things up by becoming more active at the wrong time. Rule No. 1 is transformed when you're able to think in terms of years and decades instead of months or quarters.

Of course, this means you have to have a handle on your risk profile and time horizon so you're able to assess how much money is reasonable to put at risk in stocks based on your personal situation.

The Risk Tolerance Questionnaire

Building a portfolio always comes down to determining your ability, willingness, and need to take risk. This is true for institutional and individual investors alike. If I had to boil down a risk tolerance questionnaire into two simple questions, here's what I would ask:

1. When do I need the money?
2. How much can I afford to lose in the meantime, both mentally and financially?

Every other decision more or less branches off from these two questions. The problem is that even if you're able to determine the answers to these two questions, it's difficult to keep the same attitude about risk when the markets are in a constant state of change. Your perception of these market and economic events is also sure to change depending on a number of factors, including past experiences with the markets, as well as your current circumstances. Everyone becomes a bull during rising markets and a bear during falling markets. Even if your circumstances don't change much, your perception of risk will be all over the map as the markets move. Studies show that we humans are terrible at forecasting how we're going to feel during future situations. The actual experience of an event is normally a lot less scary than we imagine it to be. This can have a huge impact on the decision-making process.

In one study, researchers picked nine risks that included things like AIDS, crime, and teen suicide to compare people's level of concern about each risk with some objective measures about the risks. They found that people's perception of risk is all over the place.

For some, as the concern rose and fell for each risk in the media and society at large, their concern followed the same path. But for others the concern about any particular risk rose and fell for no apparent reason. There was no connection whatsoever that should have made the perception of the risk change, but it did. The conclusion of the study was that there was no relationship they could determine between actual risk and perceived risk. It's basically how each individual reacts based on their environment, personality, and experience.[3]

The same holds true for the financial markets. In another study, researchers found that cloudy days increased the perceived overvaluation of the markets for both individual stocks and the market as a whole. This led institutional investors to make more sales on cloudy days when they were in a gloomy mood. Take note if you have any investment funds based in London or Seattle. The increased weather-based pessimism resulted in a negative impact on the overall stock market on cloudy days because more investors were selling. This makes no sense in theory, which is why the markets can be so frustrating. Theory doesn't always work in the real world.[4]

Investing in the financial markets can be very counterintuitive. Lower quality companies can become bargains at the right price while high-quality companies can become far too expensive after a string of gains. Great companies don't always make for great stocks but terrible companies can become great investments at the right price. Buying things on sale makes the most sense but we can't help but be affected by declining portfolio values and decreasing net worth during a market sell-off. Investors with future earning powers and savings to put to work in the markets should be overjoyed when stocks go into a bear market, but instead investors decide stocks are riskier after they go on sale.

Aside from experience in dealing with the markets on a regular basis, something that only comes with time, there's probably not much that we can do to dampen these types of emotions except acknowledge that they exist. It's always going to feel more comfortable taking risk when there is a perceived amount of certainty (read: gains) than when there is a perceived amount of uncertainty (read: losses). Knowing that we think this way is useful when creating an investment plan because you can find ways to systematically root out the bad behavior. Acceptance is the first step.

Risk versus Uncertainty

War is the realm of uncertainty; three quarters of the factors on which action in war is based are wrapped in a fog of greater or lesser uncertainty.
—Carl von Clausewitz

The list of uncertainties in the markets is seemingly endless—interest rates, corporate earnings growth, the rate of inflation, future tax rates, economic growth, political posturing, consumer confidence—the list could go on forever. As author James Playsted Wood said, "The thing that most affects the market is everything." The list of distractions investors are forced to deal with is also a mile long—the hottest markets, the best performing stocks, continuous economic data releases, new fund rollouts, pundit predictions, your brother-in-law bragging about his penny stocks, and so on.

Charles Ellis once said, "Forecasting the future of any variable is difficult, forecasting the interacting futures of many changing variables is more difficult, and estimating how other expert investors will interpret such complex changes is extraordinarily difficult."[5] It can make your head hurt just thinking about it, but it's true. No one is ever going to completely understand the exact forces that drive the markets for the simple fact that no one can predict the future. A willingness to admit what it is that you don't know frees you up from the illusion of certainty in your prediction skills.

Risk is defined as the exposure to the chance of injury or loss. At times it can feel like you become injured when you lose money, so this is an apt definition. Uncertainty, on the other hand, is an unforeseeable event or outcome. It's easy for investors to confuse risk and uncertainty, but you have to be aware of the fact that things are always uncertain. They just feel more certain when markets are rising and more uncertain when they're falling.

Even if we understand the odds, how they're framed can affect how we view them. Our intuition will lead us to view risks differently if probabilities are presented as 1 in 100 versus 1 percent even though it's the exact same thing. Psychologists asked students in one experiment to eat fudge that was shaped like dog feces. The students knew it was fudge, but it was hard for them to get over the way it was presented. The subjects realized their negative feelings didn't make any sense, but they felt and acknowledged them anyway and had a difficult time eating it.[6]

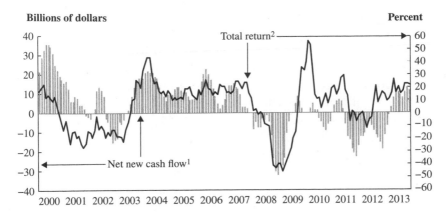

Figure 3.4   The Wrong Move at the Wrong Time

Source: Investment Company Institute.

Uncertainty is one of the leading causes of the herd mentality because it's during the times of uncertainty that we look to see what others are doing to guide our own actions. It's natural to look to others when things go wrong. Because uncertainty causes stress, our brains actively search to relieve that stress any way that we can. This leads investors to chase past performance and pull out money at the bottom of the market and put in money at the top (see Figure 3.4). It doesn't mean it's the right thing to do, but it's comforting nonetheless.

Stress is the difference between where you are and where you would like to be. It's the difference between the expectations people have for themselves and the reality they are forced to live with. This is not an easy place for your psyche to be when trying to make rational decisions. Researchers examined the stress responses of two groups of rats after they were subjected to painful electric shocks. Group 1 received the electric shocks 10 times per hour, while group 2 was shocked 50 times an hour. The second day, all rats were shocked 25 times an hour. At the end of the second day, rats from group 1 that experienced an increase in shock rate had elevated blood pressure, which is a physical sign of stress. Rats from the second group that experienced a decrease in shock rate had normal blood pressure. This works as a metaphor for the markets, because it shows how perception matters in our thought process. It's not the absolutes of good or bad that matter, but better or worse.[7] Also, those rats that had experienced much more pain were able to handle themselves better the next time pain came around.

During downturns, uncertainty results in lower prices, but once that uncertainty is removed, prices will have already risen. There's no way to predict rare events, because, well, they're rare and unknowable ahead of time. But you can predict how rare events will affect you. How will you react?

Risk Aversion

Researchers studied the stock market going back to 1952 and used the data to come up with a model that could explain the market's past movements. They found that three factors explained 85 percent of the market's moves over time:

1. The productivity of the economy, which only matters over the very long term.
2. How much of the rewards of the economy end up going to households through income, dividends, or earnings.
3. Risk aversion, which is basically how we humans react unfavorably to uncertainty.

The conclusion of the study was that roughly 75 percent of the variation in the stock market over the short term has been explained historically by risk aversion.[8] This means that emotions drive the stock market over shorter time frames but fundamentals drive the stock market over much longer time frames.

Think about that for a minute. Nearly three-quarters of the time the stock market is basically trading based on nothing more than human emotions. This is trillions of dollars in wealth trading hands every single day by some of the most intelligent people in the world. But that's what happens when we allow our feelings to take over. The prospect of making or losing money can cause people to act in bizarre ways. In fact, brain scans show that the brain activity of a person that's making money on their investments is indistinguishable from a person who is high on cocaine or morphine. Making money literally makes us feel like we are taking drugs. This is why at times it seems like the market is high (sorry, I couldn't help myself), but eventually crashes once the drugs wear off.

This becomes an increasingly important issue to deal with because the effects of the drug don't last forever. Similar studies have shown that getting exactly what you planned for is basically a non-event for your brain activity. Reaching your goals or making money on your investments should be a satisfying feeling, at least in theory. In reality, it doesn't do much for our brains if we're already planning on something. We need a bigger hit of adrenaline each time to get a bigger fix for the same emotional response. This can cause us to increase our risk to get that response. In a way, our brains are begging us to speculate, instead of invest, exactly what you don't want to be doing with your life savings on the line.

It's not only gains that can have a profound physical effect on our psyche. Losses are even worse because they're processed in the same area of the brain that responds to mortal danger. Some people literally relive their financial losses in their sleep.[9] This helps explain why losses hurt so much more than gains feel good. This can be a huge problem for our long-term financial health if we let the mortal danger signal take over during a panic in the markets.

Study after study has shown that we regret losses two to two-and-a-half times more than gains make us feel good.[10] Just think about how terrible you feel after going to the casino and losing money. It always stings way more than the great feeling you get when you win some cash. The same rings true for your favorite sports teams. Every diehard fan remembers the one that got away or the gut-punch loss to your bitter rival at the last second. No one ever forgets about the tough losses. It's always easier to recall heartbreak than successes.

This is why investors constantly obsess over market crashes. Read enough market history and you are bound to come across the following events at some point: the 1929 to 1932 crash that saw stocks fall in excess of 80 percent; the 1987 Black Monday crash that saw stocks fall over 20 percent in a single day; the technology bubble and bust that saw the NASDAQ fall over 80 percent from the peak in 2000 and the great financial crisis of 2007 to 2009 that cut nearly every stock market in the world in half or worse. Market crashes leave lasting scars that make it difficult to move on and get over them.

In 1987 the stock market had its largest one day crash ever, with the S&P 500 falling more than 20 percent. In the three days leading up to Black Monday, the market was down more than 10 percent. So in just four days, the stock market fell in excess of 30 percent! In hindsight, this was a gift for investors as a buying opportunity, as stocks went on to more than double over the following five years. It would be a mistake to think that investing or staying the course during such times of stress would have been easy. You can't simulate the fear and anguish that grips your body and mind during a crash like this when money is going down the drain. A reader of my blog shared his experience with the 1987 crash that highlights how terrifying a market crash can be.

> As one who was actually invested in 1987 (and since 1973), I still have vivid memories of that market crash. It is oh-so-easy to look today at a long-term chart having a tiny blip and say "So what! . . . of course the market recovered . . . those who sold were fools."
>
> In 1987, market news was nothing like it is today. We had no Internet. We had the next day's *WSJ* and Friday's 30-minute Lou Rukeyser's *Wall Street Week*; we subscribed to a few stock newsletters (delivered by snail mail) and *Kiplinger* and *Money* magazines . . . that's about it.
>
> Therefore, though I heard about the crash on the radio as I drove home from work on Black Monday, I was not prepared to find my wife in tears . . . her first words were "You've lost our retirement!" (Reading it does not convey the impact of hearing it.)
>
> In real time, the crash was a VERY big event. Fear for a changed future was the natural response. Talking heads were saying "This worldwide event could last for years; our children will have a lower standard of living than we have."
>
> Long story short—she insisted we sell everything the next day (which was also a significant down day); we eventually re-entered the market.[11]

It's worth pointing out that the market finished in positive territory in 1987, even after this enormous crash, but the psychological damage was done. This was something that happened almost 30 years ago, yet this gentleman had a vivid recollection of the crash to this day. You get the sense that it still brings up bad memories. This will never change either. Market crashes are never going to go away whether we like it or not, because human nature causes them. Always has, always will.

A market crash is actually one of the best things that can happen to a long-term investor because you get to buy stocks at lower prices, higher dividend yields, and lower valuations. But it's one of the scariest things you can do as an investor because you're never going to be able to buy at the exact bottom of the market and it will always feel like things could continue to get worse.

If you bought at the top of the market in September 1929 and held on until 1960 your return would have been 7.8 percent per year. If you had the nerve—or capital left—to buy in June 1932 after the 85 percent plunge in stocks and held on until 1960, you would have earned 15.9 percent annually. In both cases a long holding period resulted in positive results. But the performance can be stunning if you have your wits about you during a market crash. Starting in 1929, $1 invested turned into $9.65. Investing in 1932 turned $1 into $58.05.[12]

Each of these examples demonstrates the importance of understanding your time horizon when making investments. For example, if you look at the overall stock market on a daily basis, it's basically a flip of the coin between seeing a positive or negative return. Historically, 53 percent of all days have been positive and 47 percent negative. With our understanding of loss aversion, the fact that losses hurt more than twice as much as gains make us feel good, if you check the value of your portfolio every single day you're likely to feel terrible about the stock market every single day. Every good feeling you get from gains will get completely wiped out by the terrible feelings on the down days. Loss aversion could also mean that most people are twice as likely to make bone-headed decisions when markets fall because of those feelings. But lengthen your time horizon and the effects of loss aversion slowly start to fade. On an annual basis stocks are up roughly three out of every four years. Go out to five years and the winning percentage jumps to almost 90 percent. And going out to 20 years, U.S. stocks have shown positive returns over all 20-year periods historically.[13]

The more often you check the market value of your portfolio, the more likely it is that you'll see losses. Richard Thaler, a behavioral economist who has spent his career studying these types of investor problems, laid out the simple, yet difficult, solution when he said, "The attractiveness of the risky asset depends on the time horizon of the investor. An investor who is prepared to wait a long time before evaluating the outcome of the investment as a gain or a loss will find the risky asset more attractive than another investor who expects to evaluate the outcome soon."[14]

The Cycle of Fear and Greed

While the average long-term returns on the stock market look great, there is nothing average about market cycles. Because investors have a nasty habit of extrapolating the recent past indefinitely into the future, the pendulum always swings too far in either direction. Greed takes over during bull markets while fear grabs control during bear markets. Take a look at Table 3.3 to see just how cyclical the markets can be.

Following the Great Depression, investor appetite for risk was severely depressed. The period from the late 1920s until the end of World War II was marked by low returning, highly volatile markets. This cycle of fear, risk aversion, and volatility set the stage for the bull market that followed in the 1950s and 1960s. Greed and unreasonable expectations for the Nifty Fifty large-cap growth stocks eventually put an end to the fun just in time for the 1970s market environment, which saw highly inflationary periods that were unforgiving for stock investors. Investors began to give up on the stock market following this difficult period, just in time for the bull market of the 1980s and 1990s to begin. These two decades witnessed astronomical performance numbers with much lower than average volatility to boot, an investor's dream scenario. Of course, this period set the stage for the horrible 2000s, which were brought on by the overwhelming greed that finally reached its breaking point by the end of 1999.

I think you get the point. Fear and greed take turns running the markets as periods of above-average performance are invariably followed by periods of below-average performance and vice versa. This becomes an issue when investors allow their expectation to get out of

Table 3.3   The Cycle of Fear and Greed (S&P 500)*

	Annual Returns	Annual Volatility
1928–1945	4.6%	28.7%
1946–1968	12.9%	16.9%
1969–1977	2.9%	20.3%
1978–1999	17.2%	12.5%
2000–2008	−3.6%	20.1%
2009–2013	17.7%	11.5%

*S&P 500 Performance.

sync with reality. The optimists have won over time and the long-term trend has been up, but it's never quite as easy as it seems when simply looking back at the long-term average return numbers. Stocks have to go through these alternating periods of love and hate to earn their risk premium over bonds and cash over time.

It takes an analytical mind along with an unemotional attitude to be able to buy stocks after they've fallen substantially or gone through a prolonged sideways period. For investors with a mature portfolio, the markets like 1928 to 1945, 1969 to 1977, and 2000 to 2008 can be especially challenging. But for those who have a decade or more until they will need to spend down their portfolio and have future earnings power to save money over time, these terrible market environments are a blessing. In extremely volatile, low-returning markets, savers are consistently being offered stocks at lower prices. Some environments are better for investors while others favor savers. How you view each particular cycle will probably be determined by the maturity of your portfolio. There are silver linings in even the worst markets if you can keep your cool and continue to add to your holdings.

For most investors, it can be difficult to have this attitude since it's so scary to invest in falling markets. Every time we are in the throes of a bull market it seems everyone becomes a long-term buy-and-hold investor. The Johnny-come-lately investors say they'll never worry about losses or volatility because they're in it for the long haul. Unfortunately, once the unavoidable bear market rears its ugly head, investors get scared and sell once they've experienced losses. "I'm in for the long haul" quickly becomes "get me out I can't take it anymore." Wash, rinse, and repeat and you should be able to understand how the cycle of fear and greed persists. Gains during a rising market make everyone feel like a genius. You start to get the sense that you can do no wrong when everything you buy goes up. Overconfidence sets in and as they say, "Pride cometh before the fall." That confidence gets shattered once the good times finally come to an end. Greed quickly turns into fear. Depending on the length of the cycle of the severity of the crash, investors can be scarred by these experiences for a very long time.

The reason it's so important to understand your time horizon when investing is because when stocks fall, it can take some time for them to regain their previous levels. Going back to the 1920s, the average recovery time for bear markets in the S&P 500 is around

40 months, including reinvested dividends and accounting for inflation. So it has taken roughly three and a half years to break even after a loss of 20 percent or greater. Since World War II, the longest it's taken the stock market to recover its initial investment was five years and eight months, which occurred following the tech bust in 2000.[15]

Risk is context dependent and can change depending on your personal circumstances and your perception of risk. For most investors, your biggest risk comes from not knowing what you're doing, which means you don't have an investment plan in place. Without a plan, volatility and uncertainty will eat you alive.

Key Takeaways from Chapter 3

- It's impossible to earn higher returns over the long term in the capital markets without subjecting yourself to the possibility of loss in the short term. You can have safety of principal in the short term but it comes at the expense of long-term gains. The only way to beat inflation over time is to take risk.
- Risk means different things to different people. It's context dependent and is mostly based on your unique risk profile and time horizon. Pay attention very closely to these two variables whenever you're making an investment decision. For most investors, risk comes down to having no investment plan in place and generally having no idea what you're doing.
- Volatility can be both a risk and an opportunity, depending on how you react to market fluctuations. Intelligent investors view volatility as an opportunity, to both profit and keep their cool under pressure by following their process.

Notes

1. Potter Stewart, Jacobellis v. Ohio 378 U.S. 184 (1964), https://supreme.justia.com/cases/federal/us/378/184/case.html.
2. Stock, bond, and cash returns courtesy of NYU and A. Damadoran, http://pages.stern.nyu.edu/~adamodar/New_Home_Page/datafile/histretSP.html.
3. Dan Gardner, *The Science of Fear: How the Culture of Fear Manipulates Your Brain* (New York: Plume, 2009).
4. William N. Goetzmann, Dasol Kim, Alok Kumar, and Qin "Emma" Wang, "Weather-Induced Mood, Institutional Investors, and Stock

Returns," Social Science Research Network, September 8, 2014, http://papers.ssrn.com/sol3/papers.cfm?abstract_id=2323852.

5. Charles D. Ellis, "The Rise and Fall of Performance Investing," *Financial Analysts Journal* 70, no. 4, www.cfapubs.org/doi/pdf/10.2469/faj.v70.n4.4.

6. Gardner, *The Science of Fear.*

7. Richard Peterson, *Inside the Investor's Brain: The Power of Mind Over Money* (Hoboken, NJ: John Wiley & Sons, 2007).

8. Daniel Greenwald, Martin Lettau, and Sydney Ludvigson, "The Origins of Stock Market Fluctuations," NBER Working Paper No. 19818, January 2014.

9. Jason Zweig, *Your Money and Your Brain: How the New Science of Neuroeconomics Can Help Make You Rich* (New York: Simon & Schuster, 2008).

10. Daniel Kahneman, *Thinking, Fast and Slow* (New York: Farrar, Straus and Giroux, 2011).

11. Ben Carlson, "Would a Repeat of the 1987 Crash Really Be That Bad?" *A Wealth of Common Sense,* http://awealthofcommonsense.com/repeat-1987-crash-really-bad/.

12. William Bernstein, *The Four Pillars of Investing: Lessons for Building a Winning Portfolio* (New York: McGraw-Hill, 2010).

13. Kenneth Fisher, *The Little Book of Market Myths: How to Profit by Avoiding the Investment Mistakes Everyone Else Makes* (Hoboken, NJ: John Wiley & Sons, 2013).

14. Michael Mauboussin, *More Than You Know: Finding Financial Wisdom in Unconventional Places* (New York: Columbia University Press, 2007).

15. Jeremy Siegel, *Stocks for the Long Run: The Definitive Guide to Financial Market Returns & Long-Term Investment Strategies,* 5th ed. (New York: McGraw-Hill, 2013).

CHAPTER 4

Market Myths and Market History

*Investment wisdom begins with the realization that long-term
returns are the only ones that matter.*

—William Bernstein

Meet Bob.

Bob is the world's worst market timer.

What follows is Bob's tale of terrible market timing purchases in
the stock market.

Bob began his career in 1970 at age 22. He was a diligent saver
and planner. Bob mapped out his entire future savings in advance to
plan for retirement. His plan was to save $2,000 a year during the
1970s and bump up that amount by $2,000 each decade until he
could retire at age 65 by the end of 2013. See Table 4.1 for Bob's
saving schedule.

He started out by saving the $2,000 a year in his bank account
until he had $6,000 to invest by the end of 1972. While Bob was a dili-
gent saver, his investment skills left a lot to be desired. Bob's problem
as an investor was that he only had the courage to put his money to
work in the market after a huge run up.

All of his money went into an S&P 500 index fund at the end
of 1972.[1] The market proceeded to drop nearly 50 percent in the
1973 to 1974 bear market, so Bob put his money in at the peak of the
market right before a crash—terrible timing on his part. Although
he had terrible timing on his buy decision, Bob did have one saving
grace. Once he was in the market, he never sold his fund shares. He

63

Table 4.1   Bob's Retirement Saving's Schedule*

Decade	Annual Savings	Total Saved
1970s	$2,000	$20,000
1980s	$4,000	$40,000
1990s	$6,000	$60,000
2000s	$8,000	$80,000
2010s	$10,000	$40,000

*Bob retired in 2013.

held on for dear life because he was too nervous about being wrong on his sell decisions, too.

Remember this decision, because it's a big one.

Bob didn't feel comfortable about investing again until August 1987, after another huge bull market had taken hold. After 15 years of saving he now had $46,000 in additional funds to put to work. Again he invested in an S&P 500 index fund and again he top-ticked the market just before another crash. This time stocks lost more than 30 percent in short order right after Bob bought his index shares. Timing wasn't on Bob's side so he continued to keep his money invested just as he did before.

After the 1987 crash Bob didn't feel right about putting his future savings back into stocks until the tech bubble really ramped up by the end of 1999. He now had another $68,000 of savings to put to work. This time his purchase, at the end of December 1999, was just before a 50 percent-plus downturn that lasted until 2002. This buy decision left Bob with some more scars but he decided to make one more big purchase with his savings before he retired.

The final investment was made in October 2007, when he invested $64,000, which he had been saving since his last purchase in 2000. He rounded out his string of horrific market timing calls by buying right before another 50 percent-plus crash from the real estate bubble. After the financial crisis he decided to continue to save his money in the bank (another $46,000) but kept his stock investments in the market until he retired at the end of 2013.

To recap, Bob was a terrible market timer with his only stock market purchases being made at the market peaks just before extreme losses. Table 4.2 lists the purchase dates, the crashes that followed, and the amount invested at each date.

Table 4.2   Bob's Mistiming of Market Peaks

Date of Investment	Amount Invested	Subsequent Crash
December 1972	$6,000	–48%
August 1987	$46,000	–34%
December 1999	$68,000	–55%
October 2007	$64,000	–57%

Luckily, while Bob couldn't time his buys, he never sold out of the market even once. He didn't sell after the bear market of 1973–1974, or the Black Monday crash in 1987, or the technology bust in 2000, or the financial crisis of 2007–2009. He never sold a single share.

So how did he do?

Even though he only bought at the very top of the market, Bob still ended up a millionaire with $1.1 million. How could that be you might ask?

First of all Bob was a diligent saver and planned out his savings in advance. He never wavered on his savings goals and increased the amount he saved over time. Second, he allowed his investments to compound through the decades by never selling out of the market over his 40-plus years of investing. He gave himself a really long runway. He did have to endure a huge psychological toll from seeing large losses and sticking with his long-term mindset, but I like to think Bob didn't pay much attention to his portfolio statements over the years. He just continued to save and kept his head down.

Obviously, it's difficult to believe that Bob would have had enough intestinal fortitude to hold his stocks without selling if he was that bad of a market timer. But the point is that with a long enough time horizon, even bad decisions can get smoothed out by compound interest. Now can you imagine if Bob had simply dollar cost averaged his money into the market over this same time frame instead of constantly making bad market timing decisions? If he wouldn't have been so afraid to make purchase until he was confident in the market he would have ended up with nearly $2.3 million.

But then he wouldn't be considered "Bob, the world's worst market timer."

Bob is a prime example of the first myth about investing.

Myth 1: You Have to Time the Market to Earn Respectable Returns

Over the past 90 years or so, the U.S. stock market is up nearly 10 percent per year. That number includes periods of high market valuations and low valuations and rising and falling inflation, with short-term interest rates as high as 15 percent and as low as 0 percent. It includes many manias and panics, including the Great Depression, a recession roughly every five years, World War II, the tech bubble, and nearly one hundred 10 percent corrections.

Over a very long time horizon a well-timed investment might not matter all that much in the grand scheme of things. Legendary mutual fund manager Peter Lynch performed a study with Fidelity Investments that looked at the 30-year period from 1965 to 1995 and found that if you invested every single year at the lows in the market (the lowest day to be precise) you would have earned a return of 11.7 percent annually.

Had you been the unlucky sort, the Jackie Gleasons of the world as Lynch put it, and picked the high day every single year to put your money to work, your return would have been 10.6 percent. On the other hand if you would have kept it simple and put your money to work on the first day of the year and not tried to guess one way or the other, you would have earned 11.0 percent per year. The odds of consistently picking the best and worst days are minimal, but putting money into the markets on a periodic basis is something every investor can do. So much time and energy is put into trying to figure out the best time to invest when a simple dollar cost averaging (DCA) plan with a long time horizon is much less stressful and easier to implement.[2]

There was another study done that looked at 237 market-timing newsletters. These newsletters send buy and sell signals to their paying customers. The results of the study found that the market timing calls were right less than 25 percent of the time.

It's not so much that market timing is completely impossible to pull off. Investors have done it before. Not many, but a few have done it. It's just that it's brutal psychologically. If you're making a binary choice between being completely in the market or completely out of the market it can be emotionally draining.

This is because timing the market requires two decisions—both a sale at a relatively high point and then a buy at a relatively lower point. Even if you're able to get half of that equation right (the sale), it will be extremely difficult to make yourself buy back in after stocks fall. Sitting in cash is the best feeling in the world when markets correct or crash. Talking yourself out of getting back in is much easier than pulling the trigger and going all-in again. Unless you have a systematic, rules-based process that gives you buy and sell signals that you can follow through thick and thin, it will be very difficult to force yourself to change positions when you should by using fundamentals or your gut instinct alone.

Of course, any long-term strategy can be emotionally draining at times. The trick is finding the one that balances your ability to sleep at night with a high probability of achieving your long-term financial aspirations.

Myth 2: You Have to Wait until Things Get Better Before You Invest

"I'll just wait until things start to improve before I put my money back to work in the markets." I heard variations of this line of thinking by countless investors during the market crash of 2007–2009. The problem is that if you wait for things to get better you'll end up missing the majority of the gains when markets finally come back to life.

The stock market anticipates future events and discounts them today. It doesn't always get them correct, but that's never stopped investors from trying. Markets don't usually perform the best when they go from good to great. They actually show the best performance when things go from terrible to not-quite-so-terrible as before. And it's not the absolute level of improvement that matters—it's whether things are getting better or worse. If things are just getting less worse, investors perceive this as a positive because there's nowhere to go but up.

For example, since 1950 the average unemployment rate is just over 6 percent. When the unemployment rate has been below average, the S&P 500 is up 6 percent annually, much lower than the long-term average of almost 10 percent per year in that time. When the unemployment rate has been above average, the annual performance of stocks jumps to over 16 percent per year. An unfortunate truth of the stock market is that the best time to buy is when conditions are at their worst.

Table 4.3   Unemployment Rate and Stock Market Returns

Unemployment Rate	S&P 500 Annualized Returns	Frequency
>9%	24.50%	8%
7%–9%	15.10%	22%
5%–7%	8.30%	47%
<5%	3.90%	24%

Source: Federal Reserve.

Breaking down this relationship even further, Table 4.3 shows the returns by different unemployment rates, the corresponding stock market returns, and the frequency with which those rates were observed. When things seem the worst, it's actually the best time to invest. If you wait for things to get better, chances are the ship has already sailed.[3]

Myth 3: If Only You Can Time the Next Recession, You Can Time the Stock Market

Since 1928, the U.S. economy has been in a recession on average one out of every five years or 20 percent of the time. In that time, the longest the economy has ever gone between recessions is 10 years, from 1991 to 2001. Recessions can be painful, but somehow every time we're in the midst of a strong economic recovery, people forget that they're a natural outcome in the ebb and flow of the business cycle. Table 4.4 shows how common recessions are in the United States.

The stock market is cyclical just like the economy, so most would assume that large losses in the stock market should coincide with a contraction in GDP growth. If only it were that easy. According to Professor Jeremy Siegel, since World War II, there have been 13 instances where the Dow Jones Industrial Average fell at least 10 percent without the economy experiencing a recession (see Table 4.5). That means the market has fallen an average of 20 percent every five years or so without the economy going into a recession.[4]

The stock market and the economy are rarely in sync with one another. Economic growth tells us very little about where the stock market is going next. Over a one-year period the relationship

Table 4.4   U.S. Recessions since 1929

Recession	GDP Contraction
August 1929–March 1933	−26.7%
May 1937–June 1938	−18.2%
February–October 1945	−12.7%
November 1948–October 1949	−1.7%
July 1953–May 1954	−2.6%
August 1957–April 1958	−3.7%
April 1960–February 1961	−1.6%
December 1969–November 1970	−0.6%
November 1973–March 1975	−3.2%
January1980–July 1980	−2.2%
July 1981–November 1982	−2.7%
July 1990–March 1991	−1.4%
March 2001–November 2001	−0.3%
December 2007–June 2009	−4.3%

Source: National Bureau of Economic Research.

between GDP growth and stock market returns is next to nothing (a correlation of 0.01 where 0 implies no relationship between the data and 1.0 implies a perfect relationship between movements in the data). Even looking out over a 10-year period there's not a close relationship between the two (a correlation of just 0.05).[5] Repeat the following mantra to yourself on a consistent basis: The stock market is not the economy, the stock market is not the economy. . . .

Table 4.5   Stocks Fall 10 Percent or More with No Recession

1946–1947	−23.2%
1961–1962	−27.1%
1966	−22.3%
1967–1968	−12.5%
1971	−16.1%
1978	−12.8%
1983–1984	−15.6%
1987	−35.1%
1997	−13.3%
1998	−19.3%
2002	−31.5%
2010	−13.6%
2011	−16.8%

Source: Stocks for the Long Run.

Myth 4: There's a Precise Pattern in Historical Market Cycles

Famed value investor John Templeton once stated, "The investor who says, 'This time is different,' when in fact it's virtually a repeat of an earlier situation, has uttered among the four most costly words in the annals of investing."[6] Many investors take this quote to mean that if they can only deconstruct the historical nature of the markets they can come up with the perfect formula to figure out how it should work in the future. The problem with this line of thinking is that past cycles are completely unique. Take a look at Table 4.6, which shows various market and economic data points broken out by the different decades.

Try to find a pattern among those numbers. You will find no rhyme or reason from one decade to the next. There's no single indicator or variable that's going to give investors an edge. The only constant in the markets is the fact that they're cyclical. Nothing goes in one direction forever. As Oaktree's Howard Marks puts it, "Every once in a while, an up-or down-leg goes on for a long time and/or to a great extreme and people start to say 'this time it's different.' They cite the changes in geopolitics, institutions, technology or behavior that have rendered the 'old rules' obsolete. They make investment decisions that extrapolate the recent trend. And then it turns out that the old rules do still apply, and the cycle resumes. In the end,

Table 4.6   Every Cycle Is Unique

	Average Dividend Yield	Earnings Growth	Nominal GDP Growth	Inflation Rate	Average 10-Year Yield	Stock Returns	Bond Returns
1930s	5.5%	−5.7%	−1.4%	−2.1%	2.9%	−0.9%	4.0%
1940s	5.7%	9.9%	11.2%	5.6%	2.3%	8.5%	2.5%
1950s	4.9%	3.9%	6.3%	2.0%	3.0%	19.5%	0.8%
1960s	3.2%	5.5%	6.6%	2.3%	4.7%	7.7%	2.4%
1970s	4.0%	9.9%	9.7%	7.1%	7.5%	5.9%	5.4%
1980s	4.2%	4.4%	8.3%	5.5%	10.6%	17.3%	12.0%
1990s	2.4%	7.7%	5.6%	3.0%	6.7%	18.1%	7.4%
2000s	1.8%	0.6%	3.9%	2.6%	4.5%	−1.0%	6.3%
2010s	2.0%	17.2%	2.1%	2.1%	2.5%	15.7%	4.2%

Source: Robert Shiller.

trees don't grow to the sky, and few things go to zero. Rather, most phenomena turn out to be cyclical."[7]

But Marks and Templeton aren't talking about finding reliable indicators to be able to predict future market movements. It's human nature that's the constant in the equation. As Jesse Livermore stated more than a century ago, "Another lesson I learned early is that there is nothing new in Wall Street. There can't be because speculation is as old as the hills. Whatever happens in the stock market today has happened before and will happen again."[8] People will always fall for the trappings of fear and greed.

Cycles are inevitable, but trying to perfectly time those cycles is the hard part because, although this time is never different from the standpoint of human nature, this time is *always* different in terms of the makeup of the market. Industries change. Information becomes more abundant. Investors wise up to historical anomalies and just when you think you've found the secret indicator that explains the perfect time to buy and sell securities, it stops working.

Myth 5: Stocks and Bonds Always Move in Different Directions

Because stocks and bonds are found on different ends of the risk spectrum, many investors assume they should always be moving in opposite directions. So when stocks perform well, bonds should be performing poorly and vice versa. The usual argument is that something has to give when each are showing positive performance in the same period. This makes sense in theory, but not so much in reality when you consider that both stocks and bonds show positive gains over time. In fact, in nearly 60 percent of all annual periods going back to the 1930s, the S&P 500 and 10-year Treasuries have both had positive returns during the same year (see Table 4.7).

The relationship between stocks and bonds is anything but static, like nearly everything else in the financial markets. Over a very long time frame, these two distinct asset classes have a correlation that's more or less equal to zero—in layman's terms, this means the price movements between the two have no positive or negative relationship. Although the two are positive together most of the time, that doesn't mean that they move in lockstep with one another. Even this correlation changes over time. See Figure 4.1 to see how often the

Table 4.7   Positive Annual Returns for Stocks
and Bonds in the Same Year

Decade	Both Positive
1930s	40%
1940s	70%
1950s	30%
1960s	60%
1970s	70%
1980s	70%
1990s	70%
2000s	50%
2010s	75%
1930–2013	57%

correlation between the two asset classes is always evolving. Sometimes they're both moving up together. Other times they're going in different directions while most of the time there's no discernable pattern.

The true diversification benefit of owning both stocks and bonds comes during the down years. Going back to 1928, there have only been three times that both finished down in the same calendar year. (1931, 1941, and 1969).

Figure 4.1   Three-Year Rolling Correlation between Stocks and Bonds

Myth 6: You Need to Use Fancy Black Swan Hedges in a Time of Crisis

Following the 2007 to 2009 stock market crash investors were scrambling for answers: How can I protect against a future collapse? What kinds of funds do I need to protect myself? As usual, Wall Street was more than willing to step in with a plethora of complex strategies to fill this void including bear market funds, double and triple leveraged inverse ETFs, market neutral funds, long/short funds and a host of other fund structures that promised to protect investors on the downside. Oh, and by the way, here's a hefty fee for your troubles as we try to fight the last war for you by investing in what would have worked in 2008.

Remember, Occam's razor states that although the more complicated strategies could possibly prove correct, with no certainty about the future, the simplest solution usually makes for the best answer. Little did most investors realize that this was the case once again and we have a long history to prove it. Going back to 1928, the S&P 500 has finished the year down 24 times, or roughly one out of every four years for an average loss of almost –14 percent. Table 4.8 shows each of those annual losses, along with the corresponding returns in high-quality bonds.

In 21 out of 24 down years for stocks, bonds were up, outperforming stocks by an average of around 19 percent during the downturns.

Table 4.8 Annual Performance when Stocks Decline

Year	Stocks	Bonds		Year	Stocks	Bonds
1929	−8.3%	4.2%		1962	−8.8%	5.7%
1930	−25.1%	4.5%		1966	−10.0%	3.0%
1931	−43.8%	−2.6%		1969	−8.2%	−5.0%
1932	−8.6%	8.8%		1973	−14.3%	3.7%
1934	−1.2%	8.0%		1974	−25.9%	1.9%
1937	−35.3%	1.4%		1977	−7.0%	1.3%
1939	−1.1%	4.4%		1981	−4.7%	8.2%
1940	−10.7%	5.4%		1990	−3.1%	6.2%
1941	−12.8%	−2.0%		2000	−9.0%	16.7%
1946	−8.4%	3.1%		2001	−11.9%	5.6%
1953	−1.2%	4.1%		2002	−22.0%	12.1%
1957	−10.5%	6.8%		2008	−36.6%	20.1%

Source: Aswath Damodaran.

When an economic or geopolitical crisis hits and the stock market takes a dive, investors are drawn to the safety of bonds. They provide shelter during market storms.

During these storms, bonds act as a support system in two ways. First, they provide dry powder so investors are able to buy stocks at fire-sale prices. The only way to take advantage of lower prices is to have cash on hand to be able to buy. This requires either future savings or an allocation to bonds (or cash)—or a combination of the two. Bonds also act as liquidity for those that need to use their portfolio for spending purposes. The last thing you want to do is become a forced seller of stocks after they have fallen in value.

Second, bonds act as an emotional hedge. Bonds are steadier than stocks the majority of the time. A down year in bonds could be a bad day in the stock market. Fixed-income securities can serve as an emotional support system in the portfolio for those investors who are unwilling or unable to fully handle the periodic bouts of volatility seen in the stock market. If bonds can provide that mental barrier from making a big mistake at the wrong time from having too high of an equity allocation, then they will have served their purpose.

Myth 7: Stocks Are Riskier Than Bonds

Although bonds provide safety during times of crisis and stock market sell-offs, this doesn't necessarily mean stocks are riskier than bonds. We know from Chapter 3 that risk is a difficult concept to define. Risk means different things to different investors over different time horizons. While stock market crashes can be much more severe than bond market losses, the attractiveness of bonds over stocks wears off the longer the historical time horizon gets pushed out (see Table 4.9).

If you tally up each of the annual 30-year returns going back to 1928 for both stocks and bonds, the standard deviation, or variation, in those returns is actually larger for bonds than it is for stocks. It's 1.4 percent for stocks and 2.7 percent for bonds. What this means is that, on average, the 30-year annual returns are more variable in bonds than they are in stocks, historically speaking. So while stock returns are much more variable in the short term, bond returns are actually more variable in the long term.

Table 4.9   Percentage of the Time Stocks
Outperformed Bonds from 1871 to 2012

Time Frame	Stock Winning %
1 Year	61.3%
5 Years	69.0%
10 Years	78.2%
20 Years	95.8%
30 Years	99.3%

Source: Stocks for the Long Run.

Myth 7a: Bonds Are Riskier Than Stocks

On the flip side of this coin, there are always outlier events in the historical data. There have been three 20-year periods in the U.S. stock market where there was a 0 percent return after accounting for inflation—1900 to 1920, 1929 to 1949, and 1964 to 1984.[9] *Most of the time* is one of the most important phrases to remember about statistical relationships in the markets. Nothing works always and forever. Stocks outperform bonds most of the time. Actual returns in the markets over shorter time frames are usually far from the long-term averages. If markets were consistent, there would be no risk. And if there was no risk, there would be no risk premium earned over time in the stock market.

From 1802 to 2010, stocks outperformed long-term government bonds 71 percent of the time over 10-year periods. That number jumped to 83 percent of the time for all 20-year time frames. These numbers offer impressive odds, but you'll notice stocks didn't work 100 percent of the time. This data goes way back, but it's instructive on how cyclical the markets can be. From 1857 to 1929, there was a bull market in stocks, as they handily outpaced long bonds. Following the Great Depression in 1929 through 1949, bonds actually outperformed stocks. The relationship once again flipped from 1950 to 1999 as stocks were once again the big winners. This lasted until the tech bubble burst in 2000, when bonds were a better bet through 2010.[10] From 1929 to 1950, boring old 5-year Treasury bonds outperformed the S&P 500. From 1968 to 1980 it happened yet again.[11]

The point here isn't to assume that bonds will outperform stocks or even that you can predict when this will happen. The point is to show that there can be painful market cycles that will eventually cause investors to question every long-standing belief they hold to be true. These periods are the cause of much soul searching by investors. The market gods like to tempt investors with data that conflict with their preexisting beliefs. Just remember that long-term average return numbers are just averages, with plenty of variation around the average in the short or even intermediate term. Psychologically prepare yourself for the real possibility that your long-held beliefs about the markets will be called into question on a number of occasions throughout your lifetime.

But also remember that there is no rainbow in the stock market without a few periods of rain mixed in. It's an unfortunate but necessary precondition. Speaking of difficult market environments. . . .

Myth 8: The 2000s Were a Lost Decade for the Stock Market

Bookended by the bursting of the technology bubble and the Great Recession, the 2000s were one of the worst decades ever in the U.S. stock market. Two times the S&P 500 was chopped in half in less than 10 years. The S&P 500 suffered through this horrific decade from 2000 to 2009 finishing with a total return of –9.1 percent. That means investors lost around 1.0 percent of their money every year, on average, in the 2000s. $10,000 invested on January 1, 2000 turned into $9,085 on December 31, 2009. And that's before accounting for inflation, taxes, or fees. Many have labeled this a lost decade for stocks.

But there was a reason the returns were so horrid in the 2000s for the S&P 500. The two decades leading up to the 2000s experienced a bull market unlike any the market has ever seen. From 1980 to 1999, the S&P 500 was up a total of more than 2,500 percent or almost 18 percent per year. You read that right—double the long-term average returns for two decades. Those returns would have turned $10,000 invested at the beginning of 1980 into $260,000 by 1999.

And we all know that on the other side of a peak is the valley. Yet even though the S&P 500 makes up a large percentage of the global stock market, there are plenty of other stocks available for purchase. In fact, the 2000s were really only a lost decade for the S&P 500. Small cap stocks, value stocks, mid caps, REITs, and emerging markets all handily outperformed the S&P 500, and all had positive gains for the

Table 4.10 A Lost Decade in Stocks?*

Asset Class	Total Returns	Annual Returns
S&P 500	–9.1%	–1.0%
Emerging Markets	162.0%	10.1%
Small-Cap Value	158.6%	10.0%
Mid-Cap	84.2%	6.3%
REITs	169.0%	10.4%
Equal-Weighted Portfolio	112.9%	7.2%

*2000 to 2009.

lost decade. Take a look at Table 4.10 to see the power of diversification in action. Had you had all of your eggs in one basket—large-
cap U.S. stocks—you would have had miserable performance in that
decade. But had you spread your bets to include different subasset
classes and geographies you actually would have done pretty well.

A simple equal-weighted portfolio of the five asset classes listed
in Table 4.10 would have earned an investor 7.2 percent per year.
Not bad considering it was carrying the deadweight of the S&P 500
with it for 10 years of poor performance. We'll do a deeper dive on
diversification and asset allocation in Chapter 7, but these numbers
show how useful it can be to spread your bets and not rely on a single
asset class.

Myth 9: New All-Time Highs in the Stock Market Mean It's Going to Crash

The S&P 500 hit new all-time highs in early 2000 and subsequently
crashed by more than 50 percent over the following two years or
so. New highs were once again breached in late-2007, which was
then followed by another 50 percent-plus decline. Looking back on
this decade, many investors assumed there was a clear relationship
between all-time highs in the stock market and the risk of a future
crash. It seems every time the market shoots to new highs it subsequently gets cut in half.

Nothing in the markets is ever quite that easy. Of course, stocks
can fall from all-time highs, but hitting an all-time high isn't necessarily the trigger that causes them to fall. Since 1950, there have
been over 1,100 all-time highs reached on the S&P 500. That's good
enough for almost 7 percent of all trading days or roughly one out

of every 15 days that the market is open. Here is the breakdown by decade that shows how often the S&P 500 hits a new high level:

Decade	Number of Days
2000s	13
1990s	306
1980s	192
1970s	35
1960s	205
1950s	288

You can see that there were some droughts during certain decades. It took almost eight years to reach a new all-time high from early 1973 to late 1980. It was another seven years or so from March of 2000 to May of 2007. It took another five and a half years to reach the 2007 high, which occurred in early 2013.

This makes perfect sense when you think about it because stocks are up three out of every four years. Most of the time, stocks are rising. Therefore, it's perfectly normal for new highs to be breached on a regular basis. Of course, stocks don't have to keep going higher once they hit a new all-time high level. But it also doesn't mean that they have to immediately crash as investors have conditioned themselves to expect. A new high is not necessarily a sell signal just like it's not necessarily a buy signal. They're simply a part of a market that goes up over time, even if it incurs spectacular crashes at times.

Myth 10: A Yield on an Investment Makes It Safer

Annaly Capital Management (NLY) is a mortgage real estate investment trust company that owns real estate properties and pays out the majority of their earnings, around 90 percent, in the form of dividends to receive special tax treatment as a real estate investment trust (REIT). The share price as of year-end 2010 was $17.92 and sported a dividend yield of 15.4 percent. This is the kind of yield that can attract investors in search of income and higher returns.

In 2011, NLY actually paid out $2.44 in dividends and finished the year with a share price of $15.96. You would have earned 13.6 percent in dividends based on the 2010 year end share price, which sounds great when taken at face value. The only problem is you would have lost 10.9 percent on the stock price. On a total return basis investors netted only 2.7 percent.

The next year, the yield started out at roughly the same rate as the year before at around 15.3 percent. Actual dividends paid in 2012 came in at $2.17 while the share price ended the year at $14.04. This equates to a total return of only 1.6 percent including dividends (13.6 percent) and the share price drop (–12.0 percent). Again, not a great return considering the S&P 500 gained 16 percent.

Using the trailing dividend payouts, 2013 started out with another enticing yield of 15.5 percent. Rising interest rates caused the payout to take a hit with the company paying only $1.65 in dividends, or an 11.8 percent return of capital on the stock. The share price also took a dive and finished 2013 at $9.97, losing 29.0 percent for a total return of –17.2 percent.

This is why total return matters—not just income. The total return to investors over three years was –13.7 percent even though each year the company started out showing a yield in excess of 15 percent. Also, the amount of dividend payments dropped over 30 percent. There are investors who will see 15 percent yields and think it's a can't-miss investment opportunity with little-to-no-risk involved because there's a dividend payment attached. Yield makes investors feel safe because it's tangible. As usual, higher returns come from higher risks, and a higher yield means higher risk. Either you own high-quality investments with a lower yield, but more safety in the short term, or you own riskier investments with a higher yield and less short-term safety of principal.

The financial crisis provides a great example of the problem with using yield as a safety measure. There are a host of yield-producing assets investors have to choose from—high-quality government bonds, corporate bonds, REITs, dividend-paying stocks, junk bonds, or preferred stocks. Take a look at Table 4.11 to see how each of these income-producing assets performed during the crash.

You can see the risks involved in those income-producing assets outside of high quality bonds. How far out you want to go on the risk spectrum depends on your risk tolerance, time horizon, and the amount of psychological pain you're able to withstand during a correction or crash situation. There's nothing wrong with allocating to a riskier portion of the fixed income universe of investments. Just understand the risks ahead of time. For some, the added risk will outweigh the rewards. For others, they can withstand the

Table 4.11   Income Investments During a
Market Crash (October 2007 to February 2009)

Asset	Gain/Loss
High-Quality Bonds (BND)	6.8%
Junk Bonds (JNK)	−32.8%
Corporate Bonds (LQD)	−5.6%
Dividend Stocks (SDY)	−47.0%
Preferred Stocks (PFF)	−53.7%
REITs (VNG)	−64.1%

Source: Yahoo! Finance.

higher risk for the potentially higher reward. Investors need to understand themselves to be able choose wisely among the assets they include in a portfolio.

Myth 11: Commodities Are a Good Long-Term Investment

Want to know the best way to find your way into a financial advisor's asset allocation model? Exhibit supremely strong performance over the most recent period. Case in point is the mid-2000s commodities super-cycle that caused many investors to consider an allocation to commodities.

Most diversified baskets of commodities more than doubled in value in the 2001 to 2007 period. Precious metals equities—the stocks of the companies that extract these commodities for use—were up an astonishing 615 percent.

Seeing those juicy returns, the money poured into commodities-based funds as Wall Street was more than willing to fill the insatiable investor demand. Unfortunately, the financial crisis and the ensuing low-inflation environment have made for a difficult environment for commodities investors ever since. The Vanguard Precious Metals Fund was down 56 percent in 2008 alone. After a rally in 2009 and 2010, it dropped another 63 percent through 2014.

These stocks are not for the faint of heart. Since the inception of the Vanguard Precious Metals Fund in 1985, the annual performance is roughly 5.6 percent per year, about half of the return of the S&P 500 in that time. And for their troubles, investors had to deal with double the volatility. There could be some diversification benefits to holding such volatile stocks in a portfolio, but it's highly unlikely many investors have the stomach for that type of volatility without the higher returns as a reward.

What about investing in physical commodities themselves you might ask? Their performance has been much worse than the precious metals stocks. From 1991 to 2014, a diversified index of commodities only slightly outpaced the return of cash (Treasury bills), but with much higher risk.[12]

Unless we see a return to the highly inflationary decade of the 1970s, it's unlikely that commodities deserve a place in a diversified portfolio. Only those who can handle bone-crushing volatility and returns that are less than the stock market should apply. Generally, commodities are better suited as vehicles for short-term traders, not long-term investors.

Myth 12: Housing Is a Good Long-Term Investment

From 1930 to 2013, according to the Case–Shiller Index, housing in the United States returned 3.8 percent per year, just over the 3.5 percent rate of inflation in that time. That means, net of inflation, housing barely broke even. And these numbers don't include the ancillary costs—taxes, maintenance, mortgage interest, insurance, closing costs, real estate broker fees, and so on. Add these costs and you'd be lucky to break even on average.[13]

And when housing prices did really take off starting in the early 1990s following a mild recession, the Case-Shiller index was only up 3.2 percent per year through the end of 2013. Real estate investment trusts (REITs), commercial real estate securities that can be diversified by geography and different types of real estate—apartments, office complexes, shopping centers, and so on—were up more than 10 percent a year in that time frame.

You would think that because housing prices tend to go up most of the time that housing would be a worthwhile investment. Here's Robert Shiller, who the Case-Shiller Index is named after, on why this isn't the case:

> Here is a harsh truth about homeownership: Over the long haul, it's hard for homes to compete with the stock market in real appreciation. That's because companies whose shares are traded on a stock exchange retain a good share of their earnings to plow back into the business. The business should grow

and its real stock price should also grow through time—unless the company makes poor decisions, as some certainly do.

By contrast, real home prices should decline with time, except to the extent that households shell out some money and plow back some of their incomes into maintenance and improvements, because homes wear out and go out of style.[14]

Of course there will be those areas in big cities, waterfronts, and popular school districts that are outliers over time if you bought in at the right time and in the right neighborhood. But a house is likely the biggest asset you will ever purchase that requires a significant amount of debt in a single property that's tied to your local economy, where you also happen to live and work. It can be a huge risk to use only your home to fund your retirement. Plus there's the fact that you can't spend your house, so to speak, unless you take equity out of it.

I'm not saying that you shouldn't purchase a home because it doesn't have an above average return profile. On the contrary, a home can provide psychic income—you get to choose your own neighborhood, school district, and take pride in home ownership by putting down roots in a place that you control. Think of housing as more of an asset that forces you to build equity over time than an investment that is likely to compound your savings. On average, your primary residence is not likely to be a huge money winner after netting out all costs and the potential risk involved with putting your entire net worth into a single, levered asset. You can accumulate wealth in your home, but it's too risky to assume that it should be the only asset on your personal balance sheet.

Myth 13: Investing in the Stock Market Is Like Gambling at a Casino

"The stock market is rigged. It's like rolling the dice at a casino. I might as well just buy a lottery ticket." This is how many people felt about investing in stocks following the 2007–2009 crash. In reality, it's our emotions that are rigged against us, not the markets. While the Great Recession was an extraordinarily painful period of economic and financial ruin for many people, as investors you have to expect to deal with those types of gut-wrenching markets a few times throughout your life. Harry Truman once said, "The only thing new in the world is the history you don't know." Replace "world"

Figure 4.2   S&P 500 1900 to 2014

with "finance" and this explains the reaction of the majority of stock market investors during a panic. Knowing your financial history provides not only the knowledge necessary to remain calm during market downturns, but also helps to show that the markets have always been cyclical. Yes, they can be a roller coaster, but the trend is still in favor of progress. If anything, investors learned in 2008 that they over-estimated their tolerance for risk.

The one thing you should never be as an investor is surprised by how far the markets travel in either direction. The reasons will always be different for the rise and fall, but the magnitude of gains and losses should never catch you off guard. The reason for this is simple—people control the stock market and those people sometimes get together to make irrational decisions all at the same time. The feelings produced by bull and bear markets rarely change: nervous, excited, scared, happy, euphoric, confused, perplexed, frustrated, angry, envious, delighted, and of course fearful and greedy.

Most investment books show a very long-term chart of the stock market to prove how great of an investment stocks can be over the *very* long run. Something like Figure 4.2. If nothing else, this chart shows the power of human ingenuity and innovation over the past 100 years or so. It tells us nothing about where stocks are going, but it does tell us where the markets have been. It also says nothing about taxes, fees, or trading activity, so take it for what it's worth. But to disprove the assumption that the market acts as something of a dirty pit boss at the casino, I've always been more interested in

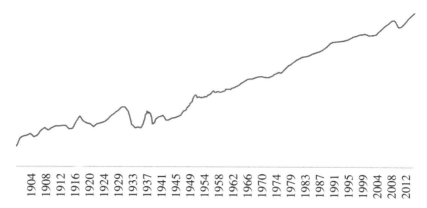

Figure 4.3   S&P 500 Dividends 1900 to 2014

Figure 4.3, which shows the historical growth in dividends on the S&P 500. Dividends represent actual cash paid out to shareholders. It's real, tangible money. Casinos don't make dividend payments. You can't fake cash payments. In fact, dividends rarely rise or fall as much as the stock market does. Between September 1929 and June of 1932, the stock market fell 81 percent as measured by the inflation-adjusted S&P index. But in that time inflation-adjusted dividends only fell 11 percent. When the market fell 54 percent, from January of 1973 to December of 1974, real dividends fell only 6 percent.[15]

The long-term increase in the stock market is entirely the result of the increase in long-term dividends and earnings growth of the companies that make up the market. How much investors are willing to pay for those earnings and dividends will change constantly. Much of these fluctuations have to do with speculation, but most of them have to do with the fact that investors are constantly projecting out the recent past into an uncertain future. That doesn't mean the odds are stacked against individual investors; just the ones who are unable to control their emotions.

Key Takeaways from Chapter 4

- Historical data is littered with caveats, counterintuitive results, and no easy answers over the short- to intermediate-term. Over the long term, the markets are much more consistent, but it requires a great deal of patience and discipline to remain a long-term investor when short-term instincts take over.

- The long-term average market performance is made up of many periods that are anything but average. Plan on experiencing uneven results, frustrating periods, volatility, and the occasional crash.
- Financial market history can be useful in defining and managing risk, but it will never be able to tell you how to make the perfect move at the perfect time.

Notes

1. The first index fund wasn't technically created until 1976, but this is for illustrative purposes only. Past performance tells us nothing about what's going to happen in the future and I don't recommend that anyone actually invest their money this way by looking for market tops.
2. PBS Frontline, "Betting on the Market: Peter Lynch," *Frontline*, www.pbs.org/wgbh/pages/frontline/shows/betting/pros/lynch.html.
3. Ben Carlson, "How the Unemployment Rate Affects the Stock Market," *A Wealth of Common Sense*, http://awealthofcommonsense.com /unemployment-rate-stock-performance/.
4. Jeremy Siegel, *Stocks for the Long Run: The Definitive Guide to Financial Market Returns & Long-Term Investment Strategies*, 5th ed. (New York: McGraw-Hill, 2013).
5. Morgan Housel, "Growing Economy Doesn't Guarantee Stock Gains," *Wall Street Journal*, November 7, 2014, http://online.wsj.com/articles/a-growing-economy-doesnt-guarantee-stocks-will-rise-1415372099.
6. John Templeton, "16 Rules for Investment Success," Franklin Templeton Investments, 1993.
7. Howard Marks, *The Most Important Thing* (New York: Columbia Business School Publishing, 2011).
8. Edwin Lefevre, *Reminiscences of a Stock Operator* (Hoboken, NJ: John Wiley & Sons, 2010).
9. William Bernstein, *The Four Pillars of Investing: Lessons for Building a Winning Portfolio* (New York: McGraw-Hill, 2010).
10. Rob Arnott, "The Biggest Urban Legend in Finance," *Research Affiliates*, March 2011, www.researchaffiliates.com/Our%20Ideas/Insig hts/Fundamentals/Pages/F_2011_March_The_Biggest_Urban_Legend .aspx.
11. Rick Ferri, "Expect Years of Pain Before Market Gains," RickFerri.com, November 28, 2011, www.rickferri.com/blog/markets/expect-years-of-pain-before-market-gain/.

12. Ben Carlson, "Are Commodities for Trading or Investing?" *A Wealth of Common Sense* (blog), August 12, 2014, http://awealthofcommon sense.com/commodities-trading-investing/.
13. Robert J. Shiller, *Irrational Exuberance* (Princeton, NJ: Princeton University Press, 2000).
14. Robert Shiller online data, available at www.econ.yale.edu/~shiller/data.htm.
15. Robert Shiller, "Why Home Prices Change (or Don't)," *New York Times*, April 13, 2013, www.nytimes.com/2013/04/14/business/why-home-prices-change-or-dont.html.

CHAPTER

Defining Your
Investment Philosophy

*Investment philosophy is really about temperament, not raw
intellect. In fact, proper temperament will beat high IQ all day.*

—Michael Mauboussin

In December 2008, as the financial world was in the process of crumbling all around us following the near collapse of the banking system and the bankruptcy of Lehman Brothers, there was another event that shook the collective trust of the investing public. Bernie Madoff's Ponzi scheme—the largest in history at almost $65 billion in fake gains promised to clients—finally unraveled after years of lies and deception.

That very same month Dr. Stephen Greenspan released a book called *Annals of Gullibility: Why We Get Duped and How to Avoid It* that focused on human competence or the lack thereof. Greenspan specializes in gullibility and foolishness. Gullibility is when our intelligence fails us and we are easily tricked into doing something that's against our better judgment. Now here's the kicker—Greenspan was an investor in Madoff's funds! The man who literally wrote the book on human gullibility was himself duped into investing in the biggest Ponzi scheme of all-time. Greenspan was kind enough to pen an op-ed for the *Wall Street Journal* to explain what caused this to happen and share some lessons he took away from the experience:

In my own case, the decision to invest in the Rye fund (a feeder fund invested with Madoff) reflected both my profound ignorance of finance, and my somewhat lazy unwillingness to remedy that ignorance. To get around my lack of financial knowledge and my lazy cognitive style around finance, I had come up with the heuristic (or mental shorthand) of identifying more financially knowledgeable advisers and trusting in their judgment and recommendations. This heuristic had worked for me in the past and I had no reason to doubt that it would work for me in this case.

My belief in the wisdom of this course of action was so strong that when a skeptical (and financially savvy) friend back in Colorado warned me against the investment, I chalked the warning up to his sometime tendency towards knee-jerk cynicism.[1]

The beauty in Madoff's scam was the fact that he never promised home runs to his investors. Over an 18-year period, Madoff claimed to offer 10.6 percent annual returns to his investors, fairly similar to historical stock market gains. But the annualized volatility was under 2.5 percent, a fraction of the variability seen in the stock market, or the bond market for that matter.[2] And what do investors want more than anything? If you answered a stock market return profile minus the stock market risk profile, you answered correctly. Investors *want* to believe this is possible. They want to take no risk but earn high returns. There were a number of warning signs throughout the years that should have caused concern among investors and those performing due diligence on Madoff's practice. But all a person needed to do was look at the performance and volatility figures to realize something was amiss.

One of the biggest issues with the Madoff case is the fact that we instinctively trust someone in a position of authority. It's easier to put your brain on auto pilot when someone else is making the decisions for you. There's a funny story about a doctor who ordered ear drops to be administered in the right ear of a patient who was suffering from an ear infection. Doctors are notorious for poor handwriting skills and using shorthand notations. In this case, instead of completely writing out "right ear" on the prescription pad, the doctor abbreviated and instead wrote "R ear." The nurse on duty received the prescription with the instructions from the doctor and promptly put the ear drops on the patient's anus. She knew it was an ear infection so putting the ear drops on the patient's rear end made absolutely no sense, but she never questioned the instructions because they came from a doctor. The patient went right along as well. No one bothered to question the misinterpreted instructions because they came from someone in a position of influence.[3]

An investor without a well thought out investment philosophy might as well be throwing their money away in a Ponzi scheme or putting ear drops up their butt, because there's no use in implementing a portfolio strategy without first understanding your investment philosophy. An investment philosophy is simply a set of principles that will guide your actions when making portfolio decisions. It's your core beliefs.

It may seem like a minor distinction, but an investment philosophy must be determined before a portfolio strategy can be implemented. It's much easier to listen to a sound bite or top-10 list of tactics than to actually set out a list of principles that outline your investment philosophy, but the philosophy is so much more important. It's how you determine your investment plan, and everything else falls into place from the broader philosophy.

The first point to understand is that there is no such thing as a perfect portfolio, a fool-proof system, a best-in-class asset allocation, just the right amount of risk to take, or the best time to buy and sell. Let go of all hope of ever finding precision in the financial markets. There is no such thing as stable relationships or rules that work at all times. Investments strategies are only perfect in a sales pitch. Your unique situation and personality type should dictate your philosophy. No style will work for everyone.

Philosophy leads to an investment strategy which leads to portfolio construction which is all worthless if you don't have a process in place that allows you to follow each of these steps. Without an understanding of your philosophy you will almost surely jump ship at the first sign of trouble in the markets or your portfolio. An investment philosophy will get its true test during a market correction or crash. Doubt will begin to seep in. Temptation to make changes to your process will slowly creep into your psyche. Defining yourself as an investor can help relieve this issue.

Degrees of Active and Passive Management

Many investors try to define themselves as having either an active or a passive investment philosophy. Active funds try to beat the market through superior security or industry selection, different factor weights—taking different risks than a market index—or timing the market. Passive funds are usually thought of as index funds and ETFs that mimic a specific market, less a small fee. There are now hundreds of different index funds or ETFs to choose from and they are so easy to buy and sell that based upon how some investors use them, you can hardly call it passive investing. There's an index for everything, so many of these strategies are active, in some respects, because they're much different than the overall markets. There's nothing wrong with being different than the market, but it makes sense to understand these differences. These phrases—passive and active— are mostly marketing material. The lines are becoming increasingly blurred between the two approaches and it's going to matter less and less in the future as the industry evolves and ETFs continue to take market share from the current crop of overpriced and overhyped active mutual funds.

To help sort out all of the clutter, here are the five degrees of active and passive investing:

1. **Total market index funds.** The classic three-fund portfolio from Vanguard (or any low-cost index fund provider) consists of some combination of the Total U.S. Stock Market Index Fund, the Total International Stock Market Index Fund, and the Total U.S. Bond Market Index Fund. These three funds are very broadly diversified and include nearly 18,000 securities across a wide range of sectors, geographies, and companies. If you really want to cover all of your bases, these funds will get you there for the most part. They are extremely low cost and give you the broader market's return, whatever it may be. An investor could do far worse than investing in only these three funds. There are ways to improve total market funds by taking more risk, but there are far more ways to perform worse than perform better than these low-cost options.

2. **Sub-asset class index funds.** Within the broader markets there are also small-cap stocks that have market capitalizations under $2 billion, mid-cap stocks that have market caps

ranging from $2 to $10 billion, and a number of other funds that include different asset classes, countries, regions, sectors, or security structures. You can slice and dice the broader markets in a number of ways to target specific corners of the market that you are trying to invest in. There are both active and index funds available for the sub-asset classes.

3. **Closet indexing.** Perhaps the worst form of active management, investors in closet indexes get to underperform, but closely track, the market and also have the luxury of paying much higher fees than index funds. It's a lose–lose proposition. Career risk can be a killer in the finance industry, so being conservative and staying close to the benchmark usually works as a way to keep your job as a fund manager. As John Maynard Keynes once said, "Worldly wisdom teaches that it is better for the reputation to fail conventionally than to succeed unconventionally." This quote sums up the world of closet indexers. I'm hopeful that the innovation we are seeing in the active ETF space will slowly weed out these types of funds, but it's going to take some time. Wall Street doesn't like to give up on cash cows so easily when unsuspecting investors are still paying them fees to invest in unnecessarily high expense ratio funds, but I'm hopeful change is afoot.

4. **Active portfolio managers.** These types of strategies will try to be different than the general market. The portfolio managers don't worry too much about sector weights or benchmarks. They are simply looking to outperform the market by looking for an edge any way that they can find it. Active mutual funds offer investors the chance to outperform the market, but the obligation to pay higher fees either way. Make sure you understand what you're getting yourself into when making active fund investments and have the correct attitude about their cyclical nature.

5. **Risk factors, smart beta, or quantitative investing.** Companies can be sorted by valuation, growth characteristics, quality, yield, price momentum, or how the stocks are weighted within an index. These are funds or strategies that actively seek to highlight or focus on one or multiple distinguishable risk factors to invest in (we'll cover smart beta and value investing later in the book in more depth). It's a slow process, but investors are finally getting more affordable active strategies

through the ETF complex. It's going to take some time, but I believe that the fund manager I spoke about at the conference earlier in the book will be proven right—ETFs are going to take over the investment industry. This is a huge positive for investors, as transparency and worthwhile investment options will increase while fees will continue to come down.

Most factor-investing strategies and smart beta funds are quantitatively run, meaning they are rules-based or systematic in nature. Most likely, this means there is no human intervention in making decisions, which takes the emotions out of the investment process. The best thing about a purely quantitative strategy is the fact that it's a systematic, repeatable strategy. There's no need to worry about a fund manager losing their touch or becoming complacent with their success. There's no ego involved, little room for overconfidence, or style drift from the mandated strategy. Good decisions are made upfront to avoid poor decisions on the backend.

This assumes that the portfolio managers implementing the strategy stay out of their own way and don't tinker with the rules just because things aren't working out in their favor. There is a tendency for all investors, quants and nonquants alike, to make changes simply because something isn't working. While it makes no sense to be inflexible, you have to expect that there will be times when things won't go your way in the markets. Plan for this in advance and make sure to understand the importance of process over outcome when selecting any type of strategy, quant-based or not.

Since many of these degrees of passive and active overlap with one another, it's worthwhile to figure out the ones that can benefit your portfolio and use them to your advantage. Typically, here are five things you should look for in a solid fund offering, whether it's an index fund, a factor tilt, or an actively managed fund:

1. It should be low cost.
2. It should be disciplined and rules-based with a repeatable process.
3. It should be based on evidence and not an investment fad.

4. It should be transparent, so you should know what's in it.
5. It should be liquid, so you don't get stuck owning something you can't get out of.

In the classic investment book, *What Works on Wall Street,* author and quantitative investor Jim O'Shaughnessy cites one piece of research that looked at 45 different studies comparing the predictive ability of humans and mathematical models. When comparing the results, the researchers found that humans lost every single time. This was true even when they had access to the models beforehand. The reason, O'Shaughnessy explained is, "Models beat human forecasters because they reliably and consistently apply the same criteria time after time. Models never vary. They are always consistent. They are never moody, never fight with their spouse, are never hung over from a night on the town, and never get bored. They don't favor vivid, interesting stories over reams of statistical data. They never take anything personally. They don't have egos. They're not out to prove anything."[4]

Daniel Kahneman found similar results in his research on the subject. Time and again, Kahneman discovered in his research that simple statistical rules are superior to intuitive judgments. This can be very difficult for many to admit. The problem, according to Kahneman, is that following our intuitions is more natural. It makes us feel better than acting against them, which is exactly what you need to do most of the time when making investment decisions. One of the reasons Kahneman gives for the superiority of a systematic decision-making process is that intelligent people are not immune from behavioral biases. Even smart people need to systematically weed out their irrational impulses, because intelligent does not mean rational.[5]

An index fund is nothing special. It's systematic, disciplined, rebalanced occasionally, transparent, low-turnover, low-cost, and low-maintenance. It's one of the reasons they're so hard to beat by even brilliant fund managers. You know exactly what you're getting. Actively managed funds can do all of these things, even if they can't exactly match the cost structure of an index fund. Instead of worrying about passive versus active, think in terms of disciplined strategies versus undisciplined strategies.

Also, there's no such thing as passive investing anyways. Indexed investing doesn't mean you can't be active, just like investing in active funds doesn't mean you can't invest passively. Even those investors that rarely, if ever, make any changes and completely put their portfolio on autopilot have to make some decisions up front. There's the target asset allocation, the fund types, asset location (tax sheltered or not), rebalancing intervals, and so on. Even the act of not making a decision counts as a decision.

In the future, simple portfolios will be extremely low cost while factor tilts will be cheaper than ever through a combination of competition and scale. Smart beta ETFs are already starting to turn a form of systematic active investing into this same type of process. But low cost and ease of access don't stop investors from making mistakes. When the cost of a portfolio or a trade becomes a rounding error, it's much easier to make changes. Emotions become the central component when costs are minimized. Behavior has always been more important than costs, but this will only be magnified as the cost structure falls. The biggest things for investors is to understand what you own and why you own it.

The Benefits of Doing Nothing

> *Lethargy, bordering on sloth, should remain the cornerstone of an investment style.*
>
> —Warren Buffett

Vanguard founder John Bogle once said, "Don't just do something. Stand there!" This is easier said than done for most people. Investors can feel lazy if they're not doing something, so people are constantly trying to keep themselves busy. There will always be a new hot investment idea that grabs your attention. Or maybe you have a model, but it's not working, so the first inclination is to make changes. It makes you feel like you did something worthwhile. The problem is that being busy all the time can be its own form of laziness. Action for the sake of action masks the fact that it's difficult to make the big decisions that are so important but not very easy. So it's the minutiae that get the most attention, even though it doesn't have much bearing on portfolio results. This makes complicated advice feel better because making unnecessary changes to a portfolio gives you that illusion of control. Being busy right now is a great excuse for abandoning a long-term process that might not matter for decades into the future.

One of the reasons that so many investors fail is because it's easy to assume that doing something, anything, is the right move in all environments. Fidelity Investments, the mutual fund behemoth with trillions in assets under management, performed a study to determine which of their accounts had done the best. They were trying to determine the traits or attributes of their investors that led to the best performance. The study's conclusions were very interesting. What they found was that the investor accounts that were completely forgotten about by their account holders ended up with the best performance. They didn't tinker with them. They didn't trade in and out of them. They simply forgot they existed so they didn't make any changes in their portfolios.[6]

Vanguard found similar results when they compared the performance of retirement investors against a benchmark that was consistent with their initial portfolio asset allocations. The investors who did nothing were more likely to earn returns similar to the benchmarks, while those who took a more hands-on, active approach to portfolio management by making moves based on market developments, tended to perform much worse. The investors who made no changes outperformed the investors who made many changes by 0.7 percent per year, on average.[7] It may not seem like much, but 0.7 percent makes up almost 8 percent of the historical average stock market return.

On the opposite end of the spectrum, another study looked into the trading activity of nearly 70,000 households. They discovered that the 20 percent of investors who traded their accounts the most actively earned an average return of more than 7 percent lower than the average household in the study. Similar studies performed in other countries have shown that these results are fairly consistent across different markets.[8] Simply put, the more often you trade the higher the probability of incurring worse results from a combination of increased costs and poor market timing decisions.

There are other side effects that can result from trying to do too much with your portfolio. When a group of researchers performed an in-depth analysis on pension funds located around the globe they found some interesting results. In an effort to diversify their portfolios by including a number of different active and passive strategies in the overall portfolio, the allocations didn't always reflect the goals and objectives that were set out for these funds. Because there were so many different factors included in these portfolios, less than one

in five said that they were confident of the various risk factor expo-
sures included across the fund. So many different risk factors were
in these portfolios that they ended up offsetting one another, leaving the funds with a neutral or market risk profile. All that work to
put together a widely diversified portfolio and they still ended up
looking like the overall market, but at a much higher cost. This is
what we call overdiversification and all it does is bring unnecessary
complexity and costs to a portfolio.[9]

The art of doing nothing most of the time doesn't mean you
can simply set your portfolio and forget it. That's not the point here
either, because that can lead to unintended consequences of its own.
You don't want to get to the point of complete avoidance or ignorance because over time your circumstances will change. You have
to save more money over time. You might reach some of your goals
so you have to spend some of your savings from your portfolio. This
would cause asset allocation changes and could require tax considerations. Just make sure you have a reason for everything you do in
your portfolio. Make your decisions contingent or if/then scenarios.
Create a barrier between yourself and irrational decisions. Make sure
there's a high enough hurdle rate before you take an action in your
portfolio. Have a set of checks and balances to go through before
making a major financial decision. Most of the time the answer will
be the same: do nothing.

Exercising Your Willpower

One of the benefits of creating a systematic, rules-based process that
does nothing most of the time is that you don't use up your limited
amount of willpower. Self-control is like a muscle. The more you use
it, the more decision fatigue sets in. The human brain can only perform at peak levels for so long. Think about all of the things people
have to deal with on a daily basis—work, children, answering e-mails,
cleaning the house and taking care of all of life's minor, yet all too
important details. Each one of these tasks uses up just a tiny bit of
willpower, but added together that muscle gets drained.

A group of research subjects were brought into a room one at a
time and asked to memorize two-digit numbers. Not exactly brain
surgery. Some in the group were asked to memorize seven-digit
numbers. Still not brain surgery, but not a walk in the park. They
were then told to walk into another room that contained some food

choices. There was chocolate cake and fruit salad and these people had to choose between the two. What they found was that the seven-digit memorizers had a much harder time refraining from eating the cake while the two-digit people had no problem at all. It was much harder for the people who were straining to remember their number to have enough willpower to be able to withstand the chocolate goodness. Their willpower was already used up on another task so they gave in to the chocolate.[10]

Another study showed that when chocolates were visible and convenient, people would eat nearly three times more than when they had to walk a short distance to get just one. You have to force yourself to find a way to create that short distance between yourself and your investment decisions.[11] Some investors constantly check the value of their portfolio. The markets are extremely random over the short term so doing this sets the investor up to take unnecessary actions. Or if no decisions are made, it uses up important willpower by resisting calls to action by the movements in the markets and the changes in your portfolio's value.

The problem with decision fatigue is that, unlike physical fatigue, you don't consciously notice when it's happening. As the number of decisions you make throughout the day increases, things eventually start to snowball until it becomes very hard for your brain to function at top speed. The unfortunate byproduct of this is that it leads to mental shortcuts. These shortcuts can lead to two irrational behaviors: Making impulsive decisions, and avoiding the difficult decisions you need to make altogether.

Impulsive decisions are based on intuitive feelings that require little thought or deliberation. In this situation, there is little attention paid to the potential consequences of our actions. It feels better in the short run, but in the long run the problems just end up compounding, making the situation even worse. Good intentions alone won't be enough to deal with this type of laziness. You have to systematically root out your own bad behavior.[12]

People like to think that an increase in their number of choices allows them to make better decisions. Intuitively, this makes sense, but our brains function counterintuitively, so more choices often times cause people to freeze up and do nothing. Researchers looked at a number of different 401(k) retirement plans and separated them out by the number of fund choices that were made available to workers in the plan. The plans that contained an abundance of fund options caused by far the most uncertainty in plan participants. In fact, the more funds a retirement plan offered, the lower probability it was that a person would take part in the 401(k) plan. So not only is it difficult to make investing decisions with numerous choices, it can be a huge barrier to start saving for retirement in the first place. It's an overwhelming feeling.[13]

A disorganized investment philosophy will eventually lead to poor results. That's fairly obvious, but even a good investment philosophy will be useless if you don't have discipline and patience to follow it over time. Understanding your limitations, including the amount of willpower, time, and energy you have to put into any investment strategy, should be a huge determining factor in the philosophy you choose to implement.

Simplicity Leads to Purity

Jiro Ono is arguably the best sushi chef on earth. His restaurant, Sukiyabashi Jiro, earned three Michelin stars, the highest honor a food establishment can receive. The three-star award means that Michelin has determined that it's worth it to travel all the way to the location of the restaurant—Japan in this case—simply to try the cuisine. The most surprising part about Ono's sushi resides in its simplicity. The most well-known food critic in Japan described this conundrum by asking, "How can something so simple have so much depth of flavor?" What is the secret to Jiro's famous sushi? According to his son, Yoshikazu, "The techniques we use are no big secret. It really comes down to making an effort and repeating the same thing every day." According to Jiro himself, "Ultimate simplicity leads to purity."[14]

Obviously, there's much more that goes into a process that creates the world's best sushi other than simplicity. But this goes to show you that getting results doesn't have to require mind-bending complexity. The benefits of simplicity, even for those who excel at their craft, is that it can help keep you grounded. This can be a good lesson to understand in all walks of life. People who earn the most money are likely to be higher up the totem pole in management positions at most companies. The problem is that the power and responsibility these higher-ups have can lead to overconfidence in other areas of their life. A study of the investment performance of this group showed that they developed overconfidence because of their management and income status, which translated into increased trading activity in their portfolios. Predictably, this led to lower than average performance in their investment accounts.[15] It can be difficult for intelligent people to realize that success in one field doesn't necessarily translate into market success. In fact, successful people are probably more prone to investing errors because they are so intelligent and overconfident. Only those who are able to recognize their limitations are able to have lasting success in the markets.

The reason overconfidence in one's abilities can lead to problems is because it always feels like the information that we have is much more important than what we don't know. Human nature causes a need for predictability and control. Once investors feel they have a sense of control and certainty over the markets and assume they understand exactly how things work, trouble strikes. A feeling of predictability is what can actually cause panics in the markets because stability can lead to instability when investors become complacent. Risk management goes out the window. Once the illusion of control is lost and everyone realizes the emperor has no clothes, panic sets in because the false sense of security has vanished. Uncertainty becomes relevant again even though it never really left. When people feel that they are in control they are willing to take on more risk and therefore uncertainty. They underestimate risk. When they don't feel in control they overestimate risk. This is why an investor must determine ahead of time those situations that cause him or her fear (losses) and greed (gains), and then create a system that ameliorates these emotions.[16]

Defining Yourself as an Investor

It's not always easy to define yourself as an investor. There are so many labels out there that it can be hard to keep up—value investor, short-term trader, index investor, active investor, diversified asset allocator, buy, hold, and rebalance, trend follower, tactical, quantitative/systematic, technical analysis, risk parity, and the list could go on. There's no right or wrong answer for every single individual. What matter most is what works for you.

There's never going to be a one-size-fits-all investment philosophy for every person. We all have different strengths and weaknesses. You have to find a belief system that fits your own personality. You can't force a square peg through a round hole just because you want to make something work for you. This will only compound your issues.

A few simple questions can help:

1. What are your core investment beliefs?
2. Do you understand your philosophy?
3. Do you know the potential risks?
4. Does it suit your personality and individual circumstances?
5. Will your philosophy help you follow the strategy you implement?
6. What constraints are necessary for turning my philosophy into a portfolio?

Regardless of the strategy you implement, the true tests of your beliefs will always come at those times when it's not working. These are the times when your investment philosophy should help.

Investor and author Rick Ferri summed this up nicely when he said, "Philosophy is universal; strategy is personal; and discipline is required. Philosophy acts as the glue that holds everything together. Philosophy first, strategy second and discipline third. These are the keys to successful investing."[17] If you want to become a successful investor, the first step involves defining your core beliefs. There's no point in trying to implement a portfolio plan of attack without first stating your investment philosophy. These beliefs should guide all subsequent portfolio management decisions.

Key Takeaways from Chapter 5

- Your investment philosophy is much different than your portfolio or strategy. Your core beliefs should guide all future portfolio management decisions.
- You don't necessarily have to choose between active and passive funds. Try to think in terms of high cost versus low cost, high activity versus low activity, and disciplined versus undisciplined.
- When designing your investment plan, systematic investing can be extremely beneficial if you are able to make good decisions up front and automate rational behavior.
- Less is more and doing nothing can be exemplary behavior, assuming it's part of your plan.
- Successful investment philosophies and investors are always tested during difficult markets.

Notes

1. Stephen Greenspan, "Why We Keep Falling for Financial Scams," *Wall Street Journal,* January 3, 2009, http://online.wsj.com/news/articles/SB 123093987596650197?mg=reno64-wsj.
2. Brian Portnoy, *The Investor's Paradox: The Power of Simplicity in a World of Overwhelming Choice* (New York: Palgrave Macmillan, 2013).
3. Robert Cialdini, *Influence: The Power of Persuasion* (New York: Harper Business, 2006).
4. John Reese, "For Successful Investors, Boring Is Beautiful," *The Globe and Mail,* September 18, 2014, http://m.theglobeandmail.com/globe -investor/investment-ideas/how-boredom-can-be-very-lucrative/article 20682565/.
5. Daniel Kahneman, *Thinking, Fast and Slow* (New York: Farrar, Straus and Giroux, 2013).
6. Myles Udland, "Fidelity Reviewed Which Investors Did Best and What They Found Was Hilarious," *Business Insider,* September 4, 2014, www.businessinsider.com/forgetful-investors-performed-best-2014-9.
7. Vanguard, "The Best Response to Market Volatility," Vanguard.com, October 16, 2014, https://personal.vanguard.com/us/ insights/article/market-volatility-102014.
8. Brad Barber, Terrance Odean, Yi-Tsung Lee, and Yu-Jane Liu, "Just How Much Do Individual Investors Lose by Trading?" Haas School of Business, October 2006.
9. Teresa Rivas, "Institutional Investors' Strategies Leave Them Uncertain About Risk: Northern Trust," *Barron's,* September 22, 2014, http://blogs.barrons.com/focusonfunds/2014/09/22/institutional-in vestors-strategies-leave-them-uncertain-about-risk-northern-trust/.
10. Mier Statman, *What Investors Really Want: Know What Drives Investor Behavior and Make Smarter Financial Decisions* (New York: McGraw-Hill, 2010).
11. Brian Wassink, *Mindless Eating: Why We Eat More Than We Think* (New York: Bantam, 2007).
12. John Tierney, "Do You Suffer from Decision Fatigue?" *New York Times,* August 17, 2011, www.nytimes.com/2011/08/21/magazine/do-you-suffer-from-decision-fatigue.html.
13. Wei Jiang, Gur Huberman, and Sheena Sethi-Iyengar, "How Much Choice Is Too Much? Contributions to 401(k) Retirement Plans," Columbia University, www.columbia.edu/~ss957/articles/How_Much _Choice_Is_Too_Much.pdf.
14. David Gelb, *Jiro Dreams of Sushi,* Movie, Magnolia Pictures, 2011.
15. Olivia Mitchell and Stephen Utkus, *Lessons from Behavioral Finance for Retirement Plan Design,* Wharton Financial Institutions Center, 2003, http://fic.wharton.upenn.edu/fic/papers/03/0334.pdf.

16. Anat Bracha and Elke U. Weber, "A Psychological Perspective of Financial Panic," Public Policy Discussion Papers, September 2012, www.bostonfed.org/economic/ppdp/2012/ppdp1207.pdf.
17. Rick Ferri, "Philosophy Differs from Strategy," RickFerri.com, June 16, 2014, www.rickferri.com/blog/strategy/philosophy-differs-from-strategy/.

CHAPTER 6

Behavior on Wall Street

Conquer yourself rather than the world.

—Rene Descartes

When you go into a restaurant you may think you are in control of what you order from the menu. I hate to break it to you, but that's just not the case. The restaurant industry has you figured out before you even walk through the door. They know exactly how to nudge you just enough to order what they want you to order. First, they try to guide you to look at certain items in favor of more expensive or less healthy options. Menus that carry descriptive names sell better and even make you think they taste better. What sounds more tempting to you: Fish eggs or caviar? Snails or escargot? Squid or calamari? Duck liver or foie gras?[1] Making a dish sound more exotic leads to higher sales as diners are actually willing to pay more for something on a menu with a fancy name. Even bolding words, adding color, or highlighting a menu item as a house favorite draws a diner's attention to those items. Restaurants even make it easier to find higher-priced items by placing them on either the top-right or bottom-left, because that's where your eyes are naturally drawn.[2]

This isn't some big conspiracy by the restaurant industry. It's just that organizations that are in the business of selling to consumers—think sales and marketing—are experts on human psychology. They know what you want better than you do. Unfortunately, one of the most talent-rich environments for sales tactics is the finance industry. A talented sales staff trumps a talented investment staff in

Table 6.1   The Number of Mutual Funds Leaving and Entering the Industry

Year	Opened	Merged	Liquidated
2003	499	394	286
2004	534	248	286
2005	708	337	251
2006	680	230	207
2007	726	315	221
2008	710	257	332
2009	501	362	508
2010	572	258	241
2011	654	300	213
2012	667	196	305
2013	660	169	255
Totals	6,911	3,066	3,105

Source: Investment Company Institute.

attracting clients. It's a sad, but true fact. The products that sound the best are often the worst ones to invest in. Increased activity does not necessarily lead to better results, but that's what you're being sold on a daily basis by most firms. The longer it takes someone to explain their investing approach, the worse off it tends to be, but the more intelligent it sounds to unsuspecting investment consumers.

The financial industry is in the business of selling complexity. They are always ready to change the packaging on existing products or close the ones that aren't working. Wall Street will try to overwhelm you with their own version of foie gras that comes with higher costs, and needless complexity. Just look at Table 6.1 to see how many hundreds and hundreds of mutual funds are both created and destroyed on an annual basis. Almost 7,000 mutual funds were created from 2003 to 2013 while almost 6,200 were merged or shut down completely.

That's not a very favorable track record, to say the least. The industry basically throws a bunch of funds up against the wall hoping some will stick, knowing that they can always close or merge the ones that don't. At the same time, there are always new and creative ways to sell new funds or products that play up to investor emotions and the recent market action. The menu is being changed constantly.

Wall Street is notorious for taking investing fads too far by creating far too many products when something shows promising performance. While some of these products will be worthwhile, you never want to get to the point that you wonder, "What was I thinking investing in this?" Jason Hsu, cofounder of the asset management firm Research Affiliates, states the opposing end goals for investors and asset managers: "So, for the record, let's say it loud and clear: Investment management is a for-profit enterprise. As such, asset managers and asset owners have a relationship beset with natural conflicts." Hsu continues, "Asset owners want fees below 10 bps; asset managers prefer "2 percent + 20 percent." Asset owners want transparency; asset managers favor black-box opacity. Asset owners want simplicity; asset managers hire rocket scientists to create complex optimized solutions for sex appeal. Asset owners want "future" outperformance after they fund a manager; asset managers would be satisfied with strong past outperformance to facilitate future asset gathering. Asset owners want a bigger alpha; asset managers would happily sell them the possibility of alpha and charge handsomely for the service of selling hope."[3]

Although Wall Street controls the menu options, investors are beginning to take notice of their sales tactics. Vanguard, the low-cost fund provider has gone from upstart to industry leader with nearly $3 trillion in assets under management. While many consider Vanguard to be mainly an index fund provider, around half of all fund options are actually active funds. Over a quarter of the assets in stock funds are actively managed. Over the past decade, 91 percent of their funds, both active and indexed, were able to beat their peer group averages. The reason they are able to be so successful is because they keep their costs so low. The average expense ratio for a Vanguard Fund is only 0.19 percent, while the industry average is 1.08 percent.[4] As Morningstar's Russ Kinnel wrote in a research report on mutual fund expenses, "If there's anything in the whole world of mutual funds that you can take to the bank, it's that expense ratios help you make a better decision." Morningstar found that in every time period they tested and with all else being equal, low-cost funds beat high-cost funds. The cheapest quintile of funds produced higher total returns than the most expensive quintile of funds over every time period in every single asset class.[5]

The performance of active mutual funds leaves much to be desired, to say the least. Over any one-year period, only about 60 percent of mutual funds outperform their benchmarks. But this is far too short a time span for investors to worry about performance numbers. Anything can happen in a given year. No one should be judged on just one year of performance because the markets are far too random in that short of a time frame. The problem is that once you start to extend the time horizon, it actually becomes even more difficult to outperform. Over 10-year time horizons, the number jumps to around 70 percent of managers who underperform. What if you extend that number to 20 years? The number jumps higher to around 80 percent of funds that underperform their benchmark. The worst part of it is that the funds that lose end up losing by a much wider margin than the outperforming manager wins by.[6]

It actually makes sense that it's difficult for most active funds to beat the market over time. And it's not because a monkey throwing darts at a newspaper can do a better job at picking stocks than an active portfolio manager, as some would have you believe. In the most simplistic terms, half of all investors will beat the market, while half will underperform, before accounting for fees. Once you take into account taxes, expense ratios, and trading costs, then it makes sense that it would be difficult to outperform a benchmark that minimizes all of these costs in a disciplined way.

But it's also true that investors are much more intelligent and informed than they were in the past. There's more competition for outperformance, which only compresses it even further. It's much harder to distinguish yourself exclusively based on your skills these days. There are thousands upon thousands of PhDs, MBAs, and CFAs looking to eat your lunch in the markets on a daily basis. This is something investor and author Michael Mauboussin has termed the paradox of skill. The paradox of skill shows that as skill improves in a given task, the variance of outperformance shrinks—meaning the range of results becomes compressed—and luck becomes more important in determining the winners and losers. Again, investors aren't getting stupider. They're getting smarter. Here's Mauboussin's take: "It's not that managers have gotten dumber. It's precisely the opposite. The average manager is more skillful than in past years. The paradox of skill says that when the outcome of an activity combines skill and luck, as skill improves, luck becomes more important in shaping results." He continues, "There is a difference between saying that the short-term results of investment managers are mostly luck and saying they are all luck. Research shows that most active managers generate returns above their benchmark on a gross basis, but that those excess returns are offset by fees, leaving investors with net returns below those of the benchmark. It's not that investors lack skill, it's the paradox of skill: as investors have become more sophisticated and the dissemination of information has gotten cheaper and quicker over time, the variation in skill has narrowed and luck has become more important."[7]

The prescription for tasks that lean to the luck side of the luck-to-skill continuum is to implement a process to drive your actions. Mauboussin adds, "For activities near the luck side of the continuum, a good process is the surest path to success in the long run." Luck matters much more in the financial markets over shorter time frames, so you're bound to be wrong if you're constantly playing in the short-run sandbox.

Threading the Needle

Now let's put some numbers and cold hard data behind the difficulty so many active mutual funds have in beating simple index funds. Let's lay out the case using historical evidence and see what this means for the investor.

Exhibit 1: Beating the Market Is Hard

There are a number of reasons why most active managers underperform their benchmarks. Most have fees that are far too high, overtrade, are tax inefficient, have a drag from holding cash balances, and mistime the market. Standard & Poor's, the research firm that happens to be in charge of the S&P 500 index, is kind enough to put out a thorough, semi-annual report on the performance of active mutual funds relative to their index benchmarks. You can see in Table 6.2 that over the past one-, three-, and five-year periods the majority of active funds have failed to keep pace with their stated benchmarks.[8]

Table 6.2   Percent of Active Funds That Underperform (as of 6/30/2014)

Fund Category	One Year	Three Years	Five Years
All U.S. Stock Funds	60.2%	85.9%	73.6%
Large-Cap Stock Funds	59.4%	83.4%	89.9%
Small-Cap Stock Funds	72.1%	87.6%	90.6%
International Stock Funds	70.0%	75.6%	74.2%

Source: Standard & Poor's.

Over much longer time frames the results turn out to be much worse than that. Consider that there were more than 350 U.S. stock mutual funds in 1970 that were available to investors. Over a 45-year period through 2014, only about 100 of those funds survived. The rest were either closed or liquidated. Fund companies don't close successful funds so you can assume most of these were very poor performers. In the end, there were 45 funds that outperformed and survived the entire period. Of those 45, only 3 outperformed the market by at least 2 percent or more. This means that the odds of predicting a mutual fund with extraordinary long-term performance numbers from this set of funds in 1970 was less than 1 percent. Those aren't great odds. This is obviously an extremely long time frame, but it's not out of the question for someone just starting out in their career to have a 45-year time horizon until they retire.

Exhibit 2: Stock-Picking Is Hard

The Russell 3000 Index covers the largest 3,000 U.S. companies—roughly 98 percent of the investable universe of U.S. stocks. Everything outside of the Russell 3000 is extremely illiquid. JP Morgan Asset Management conducted a long-term study on this index going all the way back to 1980. Here are some of their findings:

1. The excess return on the median stock since its inception versus an investment in the Russell 3000 Index was –54 percent.
2. Two-thirds of all stocks underperformed versus the Russell 3000 Index from the time they were added to the index.
3. 40 percent of all stocks had negative absolute returns, suffering a permanent 70 percent or more decline from their peak value.
4. The percentage of extreme winners in the index was in the single digits, meaning a very small percentage of stocks carried most of the weight for the remaining underperforming stocks.

These results imply that there is a very small list of winners but a massive list of losers that make up the stock market's long-term performance history. JP Morgan also listed off a number of the idiosyncratic risks that each individual company faces: commodity prices, government policy, foreign competition, exchange rates, intellectual property infringement, trade policy, technological innovation, industry consolidation—the list could go on forever. In short, stock-picking is difficult and not something that should be thought of as a hobby. Your chances of picking the winning stock is very small while your odds of picking a loser are fairly large.[9]

Exhibit 3: The Mutual Fund Graveyard

We've just shown that it's difficult for mutual funds and companies to survive over longer time frames. But even over short periods, mutual funds close with regularity. Over 15 years, a Vanguard study found that of the 1,540 original funds they looked at, only 55 percent survived the entire 15-year period. The remaining 700 funds or so that didn't make it were either closed or merged into other funds. Like the study from above, both surviving and outperforming is quite the difficult task for fund managers over longer periods. Only 18 percent, or about 275 funds, of the initial 1,540 funds in the study both survived the full period and outperformed their benchmarks.[10] In a separate study, Vanguard founder John Bogle discovered that almost half of all mutual funds created in the 1990s stock market boom ended up failing and following the technology bust there were 1,000 fund failures from 2000 to 2004.[11]

Exhibit 4: If Picking One Active Fund Is Hard . . .

Rick Ferri and Alex Benke performed a study that spanned 16 years by looking at Vanguard's three-fund portfolio of total market index funds in U.S. stocks, foreign stocks, and U.S. bonds. You can see in Table 6.3 that these broadly diversified total market index funds beat the majority of active funds in their respective categories.

Table 6.3   Index Fund Outperformance 1997 to 2012

Fund Category	Index Win %	Median Loss	Median Win
U.S. Stocks (VTSMX)	77.10%	–2.01%	0.97%
International Stocks (VGTSX)	62.50%	–1.75%	1.34%
U.S. Bonds (VBMFX)	91.50%	–0.99%	0.23%
40/20/40 Portfolio	79.90%	–1.56%	0.74%
Scenario Analysis	82.90%	–1.25%	0.52%

Source: Ferri and Benke.

But look at the last line in Table 6.3. In addition to testing the performance of each individual fund in these three main asset classes, they also compared a portfolio of the three funds. This portfolio consisted of 40 percent in U.S. stocks, 20 percent in international stocks, and 40 percent in U.S. bonds or a traditional 60/40 stock/bond portfolio, which you can see performed pretty well against its peer group. Next Ferri and Benke simulated 5,000 trials of randomly selected active mutual funds taken from the same categories at the same portfolio weights as their 40/20/40 index fund portfolio. Their results were impressive and somewhat surprising to even the study's authors. When they ran a simulation, the index fund portfolio beat the active fund portfolio almost 83 percent of the time or 4,144 times. That means 856 times or just 17 percent of active portfolios outperformed.[12]

Picking a single active mutual fund that can beat an index fund is not easy. Picking an entire portfolio of active funds that can beat a portfolio of index funds is even harder.

Exhibit 5: Smaller Upside, But Bigger Downside Risk

Ferri and Benke also ran studies that included portfolios that were more broadly diversified by including more asset class breakdowns (combinations of REITs, small-cap stocks, mid-cap stocks, emerging markets, TIPs, municipal bonds, and different bond durations). Take a look at the second and third columns in Table 6.4 from the Ferri-Benke mutual fund study. These results show a bizarro asymmetrical payoff. In finance-speak, an asymmetric payoff is one in which the potential upside exceeds the potential downside when making an investment. This study shows that this large group of actively managed funds offered investors a higher probability of loss than gain, but also a larger magnitude of loss than gain. This is a double

Table 6.4   Index Fund Outperformance 2003 to 2012

Portfolios	Index Win %	Median Loss	Median Win
3 Fund	87.70%	−1.47%	0.54%
5 Fund	87.80%	−1.10%	0.44%
10 Fund	90.00%	−0.93%	0.29%

Source: Ferri and Benke.

whammy of poor odds for the average investor trying to pick a winning active mutual fund. If you're right you win by a little, but if you're wrong you lose by a lot.

Other studies have backed up Ferri and Benke's data showing that the losing funds lose 150 percent more than the winning funds win. A few other worthwhile conclusions that were drawn by the authors of this study: 1. The probability of an index fund outperformance increased as the time period jumped from five to 15 years, and 2. Index funds outperformed on a risk-adjusted basis as well, when taking volatility into account.[13]

Exhibit 6: Persistence Is a Problem

Okay, you've made it this far. Let's say you're able to choose one of the active funds that outperforms the market over time. It's not impossible; it's just not that easy. But here comes the really hard part. Even if you find the best performing fund with a killer strategy, you have to deal with the dreaded low persistence of outperformance. Even the very best investors cannot outperform over every single market cycle.

How low can the persistence of outperformance be, you ask? A team of researchers at Dow Jones looked at nearly 2,900 active mutual funds that had been open for at least a year as of March 2010. First they found the top 25 percent of funds that had the best performance in the year leading up to March 2010. Then they wanted to know how many of those funds in the original top 25 percent stayed in the top quartile of performance over the next four one-year periods. The answer? Drum roll please . . . 2?! Cue the sad trombone. Wah-*waaaah*. Two measly funds were able to stay in the top 25 percent of performers over five straight years. That translates into 0.07 percent that could stay on top consistently, while the other 99.93 percent could not.[14]

Let's bring it all together and see what we've discovered in these exhibits. Beating the market is hard because stock picking is hard, as most of the big winners over time are in a small number of individual names. Investors are becoming more intelligent, which is compressing the availability of outperformance. You're really going to have to understand their process and make sure it's disciplined enough to survive periods of underperformance. Mutual funds close at a mind-boggling pace, yet somehow new ones are always there waiting to take their place. Picking one winning mutual fund is hard, but picking an entire portfolio of funds seems to decrease your odds of success. The funds that do outperform don't win by much while the losers trail their benchmarks by a much wider margin. And finally, if you do find a fund that outperforms you have to get used to periods of underperformance on the way there as the persistence of winning funds over time is razor thin.

So Never Invest in Active Funds?

The point here is not that you should never invest in an actively managed fund. There are just a high number of expensive closet index funds that need to go away forever. But all active funds are not evil. In fact, in the next chapter we examine some of the ways you can invest outside of the broader total market that could enhance your returns or provide diversification benefits. The point is really to show how difficult it is to find consistent outperformers in the stock market. That doesn't mean there won't be outperformers—of course there will. It's not always the winning percentage that matters, but the magnitude of the wins, as well. It really comes down to this: Can you handle underperforming for long periods of time for the chance to outperform over even longer ones even though there's no guarantee? The odds of predicting the winning active funds year in and year out are not in your favor. I'm not saying it can't be done. But the question investors need to ask themselves, with a huge helping of self-awareness, is this: Can I personally expect to pick the best active managers and funds? Risk tolerance is not only about being able to handle losses, but also the psychological pain from underperforming. One plays off of your fear and the other your greed. Both can be deadly to a portfolio or investment plan. Act accordingly and choose wisely.

As technology continues to play a larger role in bringing costs down the lines between index funds and active funds will become blurred. The factors that matter more than anything are low costs, high transparency, tax efficiency, low turnover, and a disciplined process. That means avoiding high costs, complexity, tax inefficiency, high turnover, and an undisciplined process. Whether you choose to implement that viewpoint through a traditional index fund or a more active ETF will depend on how much tracking error you're willing to accept from the market's returns. Tracking error is how different your returns are from the overall market.

Index funds are far from perfect. They're never going to be the best performer. Doubt can creep into your mindset with index funds when they lose money just like it can with an active fund strategy. You'll never pick a winning lottery ticket by investing in an index fund. You're not immune to large losses by investing in a market portfolio. But you know what you're getting with an index fund. If you pick active funds, make sure you know what you're getting yourself into. You're really going to have to understand the process and make sure you and the portfolio manager are disciplined enough to survive periods of underperformance.

Only invest in active strategies or factor tilts if you are prepared to do worse for the possibility of doing better. Plus, too many investors judge their performance over time frames that are far too short to have any significance. As the persistence data shows, even the best investors can't win every single year. Value funds are a perfect example of this phenomenon (more on this in Chapter 7). Every investor has to make sure they understand ahead of time what each investment they make could entail in terms of both returns and more importantly, risk.

While the persistence data shows that it's nearly impossible to continuously outperform the market, it doesn't mean it's impossible over longer cycles. But if you are an investor who will be constantly obsessing over beating benchmarks over short-term time horizons, then extremely active investments are not going to be for you. One of the hardest questions to answer as an investor is this: Am I anchoring to a bad investment or strategy or am I staying disciplined to a good long-term process?

Probably the biggest reason it's so hard to outperform the market, other than the fact that competition has heated up so much over the past few decades, is because most portfolio managers either don't have the requisite patience to think and act for the long term or their investors don't (it's kind of a chicken or the egg problem). Academic research and the real world results of many of the greatest investors of all-time show that there are strategies that beat the market over longer time frames. It just takes extreme patience and discipline, something not enough investors have.

The Most Important Thing

Whatever fund or strategy an investor decides to utilize, it will be all for naught if the investor cannot behave themselves. When implementing a portfolio strategy you're not only managing your investments, you're managing your emotions and, to some extent, yourself. You have to confront your own vulnerabilities and work to systematically minimize them. Try to build your portfolio in a way that will take these vulnerabilities into account. Index funds, active funds, low costs, high costs—none of it matters if you can't execute your plan.

Morningstar, a research firm that provides valuable fund data to investors, publishes a very useful piece of data that shows exactly why behavior is the most important thing for investors to focus on. They look at the annual returns over the previous 10 years based on each fund's performance numbers. If you were to invest your money on day one and hold it in the fund for the entire decade-long period, this is the return you would earn on your investment. But Morningstar also looks at the asset-weighted return, which shows what the average return that investors in the funds actually earned. The difference between these two numbers, the behavior gap shown in Table 6.5, comes down to investor behavior. It's really the difference between an investment return and an investor return. The difference comes down to discipline or lack thereof.

You can see the average gap is almost 2.5 percent per year across all fund categories. The reason for the gap comes down to all of the issues we covered in Chapter 2 on negative knowledge. Investors chase past performance. They buy high and sell low. They can't simply sit on their hands and allow compound interest to grow their

Table 6.5 The Behavior Gap

Asset Class	10-Year Fund Return	Asset-Weighted Return	Behavior Gap
U.S. Equity	8.18%	6.52%	−1.66%
Sector Equity	9.46%	6.32%	−3.14%
Balanced	6.93%	4.81%	−2.12%
International Equity	8.77%	5.76%	−3.01%
Taxable Bond	5.39%	3.15%	−2.24%
Municipal	3.53%	1.65%	−1.88%
Alternative	0.96%	−1.15%	−2.11%
All Funds	7.30%	4.81%	−2.49%

Source: Morningstar.

wealth over time. Instead they trade in and out of funds to their own detriment. It's not necessarily that people are investing in poor funds. It's that they are very good at mistiming the market and very bad at timing it.[15]

In the 1960s, when America was neck and neck in a race with Russia to get the first man into space, NASA trained the astronauts in one skill more than any other—the art of not panicking.[16] Nothing else matters if you can't control your reactions under stressful situations. Panic is a huge reason for the behavior gap that persists in investor returns. It causes unforced errors. People abandon their plans. They ignore good advice. They forget their time horizon and risk profile. It becomes about the next 24 hours instead of the next 24 years.

When Daniel Kahneman was finally honored in the early 2000s with a Nobel Prize for all of his groundbreaking research on behavioral psychology, he made a terrific point during his acceptance speech that explains why the behavior gap exists and irrational short-term thinking persists (emphasis added):

> It is worth noting that an exclusive concern with the long term may be prescriptively sterile, *because the long term is not where life is lived.* Utility cannot be divorced from emotion, and emotion is triggered by changes. A theory of choice that completely ignores feelings such as the pain of losses and the regret of mistakes is not only descriptively unrealistic.[17]

The long term is the only thing that matters as far as investment returns go, but as Kahneman so aptly points out, "the long term is not where life is lived."

Key Takeaways from Chapter 6

- There are many important facets to consider when constructing a portfolio and creating an investment plan, but none of the technical building blocks will matter if you can't control your behavior.
- Beating the market is harder than most think. It's not impossible, but it's never going to be easy. Patience and a repeatable process help increase your odds for success.
- Wall Street is in the business of fee generation. They know human nature and how to sell much better than you do. Trust,

but verify and always default to common sense if there's something you don't understand. You aren't obligated to invest in something just because it's out there. Available doesn't always mean necessary.

Notes

1. Brian Wassink, *Mindless Eating: Why We Eat More Than We Think* (New York, Bantam, 2007).
2. Quentin Fottrell, "How Menus Trick You into Spending More," *MarketWatch.com*, August 2, 2014, www.marketwatch.com/story/how -menus-trick-you-into-spending-more-2014-07-31.
3. Jason Hsu, "The Promise of Smart Beta," Research Affiliates, December 2014, www.researchaffiliates.com/Our%20Ideas/Insights/ Fundamentals/Pages/319_The_Promise_of_Smart_Beta.aspx.
4. Vanguard, "Performance Report: Vanguard Funds Shined versus Peers," December 2014, https://advisors.vanguard.com/VGApp/iip/ site/advisor/research/article/ArticleTemplate.xhtml.
5. Russ Kinnel, "How Expense Ratios and Star Ratings Predict Success," Morningstar.com, August 9, 2010, http://news.morningstar .com/articlenet/article.aspx?id=347327.
6. Charles Ellis, "Seeing Investors' Reality as Our Profession's Reality," cfapubs.org, Second Quarter 2014, www.cfapubs.org/doi/pdf/ 10.2469/cp.v31.n2.7.
7. Micheal Mauboussin, *The Success Equation: Untangling Luck and Skill in Business, Sports, and Investing* (Boston: Harvard Business Review Press, 2012).
8. Aye M. Soe, "SPIVA U.S. Scorecard: Mid-Year 2014," Standard & Poor's, 2014, https://us.spindices.com/resource-center/thought -leadership/spiva.
9. Michael Cembalest, *The Agony & The Ecstasy: The Risks and Rewards of a Concentrated Portfolio,* Eye on the Market Special Edition, www.chase.com/content/dam/privatebanking/en/mobile/documents /eotm/eotm_2014_09_02_agonyescstasy.pdf.
10. Vanguard Research, "The Bumpy Road to Outperformance," July 2013, https://pressroom.vanguard.com/content/nonindexed/7.5.2013_The _bumpy_road_to_outperformance.pdf.
11. John Bogle, *Enough: True Measures of Money, Business, and Life* (Hoboken, NJ: John Wiley & Sons, 2010).
12. Richard A. Ferri and Alex C. Benke, "A Case for Index Fund Portfolios," RickFerri.com, June 2013, www.rickferri.com/WhitePaper.pdf.
13. Ibid.

14. Jeff Sommer, "Who Routinely Trounces the Stock Market? Try 2 Out of 2,862 Funds," *New York Times*, July 2014, www.nytimes.com/2014/07/20/your-money/who-routinely-trounces-the-stock-market-try-2-out-of-2862-funds.html.

15. Russ Kinnel, "Mind the Gap 2014," Morningstar.com, February 27, 2014, http://news.morningstar.com/articlenet/article.aspx?id=637022.

16. Ryan Holiday, *Obstacle Is the Way: The Timeless Art of Turning Trials Into Triumph* (New York: Portfolio, 2014).

17. Daniel Kahneman, "Maps of Bounded Rationality: A Perspective on Intuitive Judgment and Choice," Nobel Prize Speech, December 2002.

CHAPTER

Asset Allocation

Instead of concentrating on the central issue of creating sensible long-term asset-allocation targets, investors too frequently focus on the unproductive diversions of security selection and market timing.
—David Swensen

Vilfredo Pareto was an Italian economist from the late 1800s and early 1900s. Pareto made a very simple, yet very effective, discovery called the 80/20 rule that helps drill down to the most important details in many fields of study. Pareto discovered that 80 percent of the land in Italy was owned by 20 percent of the people. He also found that 80 percent of the peas in his garden came from 20 percent of the peapods that were planted. In other words, 80 percent of the results come from 20 percent of the work. Or think of this from a business perspective. At most firms, 80 percent of sales come from 20 percent of clients. In general, you can assume that 80 percent of outputs come from 20 percent of inputs.[1]

The 80/20 rule can work in many areas of life, but it's extremely important with investment management. In the case of building a portfolio, asset allocation—how you choose to split your portfolio among asset classes—is the 20 percent input that will get you 80 percent of the way there. In fact, asset allocation may get you closer to 90 percent of the way there according to one study. Roger Ibbotson and Paul Kaplan performed an in-depth study on the drivers of portfolio performance. They wanted to know if it was asset allocation that drove portfolio performance or market timing and active security selection. What they found is that more than 90 percent of a portfolio's long-term variation in return was explained by its asset allocation. That leaves only a small amount of the variation in return that can be explained by an investor's ability to time the market or successfully choose individual securities.[2]

Of course, there's no way to know for sure how accurate this 90 percent figure is. The markets don't always play out exactly as they do in research papers. But does it really matter for the individual investor? As we've already seen throughout this book, professional and individual investors as a group have a difficult time making the correct buy and sell decisions and the track record for active mutual fund stock-pickers leaves much to be desired. Certain investors can do this, but it's a fairly small group that can do it on a consistent basis. So let's assume that the majority of investors have absolutely no control over these two factors. If you cannot control them, who cares what percentage of your returns they might make up? On the other hand, asset allocation is something you do control.

Individual stocks get all of the headlines. We are bombarded with stories on a daily basis about huge gains or losses in individual companies. There are IPOs, mergers and acquisitions, analyst upgrades and downgrades, earnings releases, CEO scandals and the list goes on. Many of these events are interesting, but that doesn't make them important for your portfolio. Asset allocation is far more important than what an individual company did on any given day. But it would be difficult for the financial media to run the following headlines day after day:

Some Asset Classes Rose While Others Fell

Diversified Portfolios Protected Investors from Company X Going Bankrupt Again

Risk Management Does the Trick as Asset Allocation Model Doesn't Get Too Hot or Too Cold

Before we get into the particulars about asset allocation and diversification, it's worth noting another piece of negative knowledge— the perfect portfolio. The perfect portfolio or asset allocation does not exist. It will only be known with the benefit of perfect hindsight. You can look back at the historical data and come up with a strategy that would have worked perfectly in the past, but good look getting those same results in the future.

Your asset allocation will never be perfect, but here's a little secret for you: no one else's will either. There will always be minor tweaks and changes you could make. New ETFs are being created all the time. Many will pique your interest. Some might even make sense to add to your mix of holdings. Just try to keep a high hurdle rate for inclusion in your portfolio. The majority of the time you should be like the pretty girl at the bar constantly turning down advances from the guys trying to hit on her. Be very selective about the phone numbers you'll take.

In fact, a search for perfection can only lead to problems. You could go through all of the asset allocation studies, Monte Carlo simulations, and optimized portfolio back-tests of performance results you can find but all they will tell you is how certain portfolios have performed in the past. While these tools can be useful as a way to gauge possible risk factors, assuming future cycles will play out exactly as they have in the past can lead to overreactions when things don't go as planned. If your goal is to create a perfect portfolio you have basically already lost because you're only setting yourself up for disappointment. There are only investment styles that fit your personality and allow you to meet your needs with a high probability for success. The real perfect portfolio is whatever approach allows you to stick with your investment plan without completely abandoning your strategy at the worst possible times. It's the portfolio that helps you eliminate any possible behavior gap that comes from chasing hot funds, buying high or selling low, and investing in products or markets that you don't understand.

The specific asset classes, funds, and individual holdings you use to put together your portfolio all matter, but they matter much less to your overall results than your ability to handle difficult market environments. Sticking to a disciplined process when everyone else is losing their mind about the market is far more important than putting together the precise mix of asset classes or stocks. Sticking to your plan is therefore the closest you will get to the perfect portfolio.

Asset Allocation Decisions

While I'm big on perspective and understanding before making any huge decisions in the markets, eventually you have to actually construct a portfolio. There are some things that do matter. Not everything can be about minimizing mistakes. From an asset allocation standpoint, here are the seven important questions to consider when making this important decision:

1. How should I divide my portfolio between stocks, bonds, and other investments?
2. What other asset classes or risk factors do I want to tilt to or add to my portfolio?
3. How different do I want my portfolio to be from the market?
4. What's the portfolio that minimizes my regrets?
5. What's my appetite for risk based on my willingness and ability to take risk?
6. How do I implement an asset allocation and turn it into a legitimate portfolio?
7. How do I determine asset allocation weights within a portfolio?

First of all, it's extremely important to have a reason for every asset class and investment within your portfolio. You need to have a reason for every move that you make. The markets are constantly tempting you to make unnecessary moves in your portfolio. When there are wild fluctuations, it feels like you have to make a move to protect yourself from harm. And when the markets are calm, it feels like you have to press the issue to make something happen. Every change you make to your portfolio should have a high hurdle rate. Good reasons rarely start with, "Because I'm nervous or excited . . ." Most of the good decisions you implement will make you feel uncomfortable. And it's not just emotional decisions that you have to be aware of when making portfolio changes. Assuming you're investing outside of tax sheltered accounts, there are tax implications with every sale you make. You have to consider trading costs and the toll that second-guessing can take on your psyche after making a move. Just make sure that all changes to an asset allocation or your portfolio holdings are within your stated investment guidelines or process. Once you start shooting from the hip is when mistakes start to add up.

Asset allocation helps investors balance out their need for gains with their ability to accept losses. See Table 7.1 to get an approximation of the losses and gains based on historical market returns and different asset allocations between stocks and bonds. If you carry an all-stock portfolio over a period of time measured in decades you can be sure that there will be at least one market crash that cuts your

Table 7.1   Visualizing Risks and Rewards in Asset Allocation

Allocation		Average Annual 30-Year Returns	Growth of $10,000 over 30 Years	October 7 to March 9 Performance	October 7 to March 9 Losses on $100,000
Stocks	Bonds				
100%	0%	11.1%	$238,210	−56.6%	−$56,600
90%	10%	10.6%	$204,825	−50.2%	−$50,192
80%	20%	10.0%	$175,984	−43.8%	−$43,784
70%	30%	9.5%	$151,088	−37.4%	−$37,376
60%	40%	8.9%	$129,612	−31.0%	−$30,968
50%	50%	8.1%	$111,102	−24.6%	−$24,560
40%	60%	7.8%	$95,159	−18.2%	−$18,152
30%	70%	7.2%	$81,439	−11.7%	−$11,744
20%	80%	6.7%	$69,640	−5.3%	−$5,336
10%	90%	6.1%	$59,502	1.1%	$1,072
0%	100%	5.6%	$50,798	7.5%	$7,480

Sources: Stock market returns are based on the S&P 500 from 1928 to 2013. For bonds, 10-year Treasuries from 1928 to 1975; Barclays Aggregate Bond Index for 1976 to 2013. Past performance is used to illustrate historical risk profiles, not to predict future returns. Also, these returns do not include the effects of fees, taxes, and commissions.

portfolio value in half. It's something every investor should plan on over his or her lifetime.

Every decision involves trade-offs, so you have to be realistic about your ability to deal with gains and losses. Filling out a risk tolerance questionnaire or looking back at past market crashes with the benefit of perfect hindsight makes them look much easier to deal with than they actually were in real time. Markets always look easy through the rearview mirror. Financial writer Fred Schwed once said, "Like all of life's rich emotional experiences, the full flavor of losing important money cannot be conveyed by literature." Unless you have lived through an actual crash with real money on the line, it's impossible to know exactly how you will react when the markets take a beating. Take your past experiences into consideration when figuring out how much exposure you can reasonably handle in the stock market.

Why Diversification Matters

In the movie *Back to the Future Part II*, Marty McFly's nemesis, Biff Tannen, travels back in time to give his younger self a copy of the *Grays Sports Almanac: Complete Sports Statistics 1950–2000*. Biff from the past goes on to use this knowledge of the future to win millions of dollars gambling on future sporting events. But in a way, it wasn't gambling because he knew exactly what was going to happen.[3] If investors were able to predict the future with certainty, there would be no need to worry about asset allocation or portfolio construction. Everyone who could predict what was going to happen could pull a Biff Tannen and put their money in the best performing names or sectors. Intelligent investors understand that this is an impossible strategy and take risk and uncertainty into account when building a portfolio.

In the absence of your future self being able to travel back in time to tell you exactly what's going to happen, investors should practice diversification. Diversification is the best way to admit you have no idea what's going to happen in the future. It's how you prepare a portfolio for a wide range of future possibilities and admit your own infallibility. Some might consider diversification a form of ignorance, but one of the best ways to minimize risk in a portfolio is to admit, "I just don't know what's going to happen. I have no idea which asset class is going to perform the best from year to year, therefore I will diversify broadly across the various asset classes and risk factors." Table 7.2 shows just how difficult it can be to choose the best performing asset class in any given year. This data shows you how fleeting leadership can be in the financial markets. There seems to be little rhyme or reason from one year to the next in the best performing investments.

Like the old Winston Churchill quote about democracy, creating a diversified portfolio might be the worst way to invest . . . except for all the others. You are always going to end up hating something in your portfolio because there are no scenarios where everything is going to be firing on all cylinders. That would be far too easy. Most investors spend their time figuring out what will happen to their portfolios if they end up being right. Intelligent investors know that they should also plan for the inevitable by asking themselves: What if I'm wrong? Diversification is the "what-if-I'm-wrong?" portion of the investment process.

Everything about the investment process is a series of trade-offs. Investing itself is delaying current consumption for future consumption. You can either try to maximize your chances of getting rich or minimize your chances of missing out on your goals and becoming poor. You have to be willing to accept periodic large losses to earn higher long-term returns. Or you have to save a lot more money to accept lower returns and decrease your chances of short-term losses.

Table 7.2 The Asset Allocation Quilt

2007	2008	2009	2010	2011	2012	2013	2014
Emerging Mkts 33.1%	Bonds 7.6%	Emerging Mkts 68.9%	REITs 28.3%	REITs 8.5%	Emerging Mkts 19.1%	Small Cap 41.0%	REITs 30.1%
Int'l Stocks 13.3%	Small Cap −37.6%	Small Cap 41.6%	Small Cap 27.2%	Bonds 7.7%	Int'l Stocks 18.8%	Mid Cap 33.1%	Large Cap 13.7%
Mid Cap 12.5%	Mid Cap −36.4%	Mid Cap 37.6%	Mid Cap 26.3%	Large Cap 2.1%	Mid Cap 17.8%	Large Cap 32.2%	Mid Cap 9.4%
Bonds 6.7%	Large Cap −36.6%	REITs 29.6%	Emerging Mkts 16.5%	Small Cap 1.1%	REITs 17.5%	Int'l Stocks 21.4%	Bonds 4.5%
Large Cap 5.5%	REITs −37.1%	Int'l Stocks 26.9%	Large Cap 14.8%	Mid Cap −2.1%	Large Cap 15.8%	REITs 2.3%	Small Cap 3.0%
Small Cap 1.8%	Int'l Stocks −41.0%	Large Cap 25.9%	Int'l Stocks 8.2%	Int'l Stocks −12.3%	Small Cap 15.7%	Bonds −2.0%	Emerging Mkts −3.9%
REITs −16.5%	Emerging Mkts −48.9%	Bonds 3.3%	Bonds 6.4%	Emerging Mkts −18.8%	Bonds 3.8%	Emerging Mkts −3.7%	Int'l Stocks −6.2%

Funds: EEM, VGSIX, MDY, SLY, SPY, EFA, AGG.

You have to be able to sleep at night, but also be able to sustain your living standards throughout retirement. You have to worry about certain spending needs in the near-term but also your spending needs many decades out. Decisions, decisions.

Investing really comes down to regret minimization. Some investors will regret missing out on huge gains while others will regret participating in huge losses. Which regret will wear worse on your emotions? Missing out on future gains or future losses? Diversification within a well-thought-out asset allocation is your best option to minimize these two regrets. You'll never go broke practicing diversification, but you must be willing to accept short-term regrets in place of long-term ones. Diversification also helps control your behavior. You never completely miss out on the biggest gains while you never fully participate in the biggest losses. Of course, diversification can't completely protect you from poor performance over days, months, or even years. You have to be able to withstand losing money at some point to be able to make money. But diversification does protect investors from experiencing numerous poor cycles or decades, which is where real risk resides. Diversification is about accepting good enough while missing out on extraordinary so you can avoid terrible. Famed value investor Howard Marks once said, "Here is part of the tradeoff with diversification. You must be diversified enough to survive bad times or bad luck so that skill and good process can have the chance to pay off over the long term."[4]

Another reason to diversify is because there is always the possibility that your time horizon will coincide with a poor performing market, even over the long term. Financial writer and investor Morgan Housel ran the numbers to see how different starting points—depending on when you were born—would affect the ending balances for retirement savers. Specifically, Housel looked at what would have happened if someone saved $500 a month and invested that money into the S&P 500 over a 20-year time frame at different starting points from 1871 to 2013. On an inflation-adjusted basis, the best 20-year period was from 1980 to 2000, which turned this periodic investment into almost $400,000. On the other end of the spectrum, the worst 20-year period was from 1962 to 1982, when the ending balance was slightly less than $60,000 adjusted for inflation, which was really one of the main culprits for the severe underperformance during this period (Isn't it interesting that the best performing period followed the worst?).[5] Both periods included

Table 7.3   Annual Returns by Decade

	Stocks	Bonds	50/50 Portfolio
1930s	−0.9%	4.0%	2.8%
1940s	8.5%	2.5%	5.8%
1950s	19.5%	0.8%	10.5%
1960s	7.7%	2.4%	5.3%
1970s	5.9%	5.4%	6.1%
1980s	17.3%	12.0%	14.9%
1990s	18.1%	7.4%	12.9%
2000s	−1.0%	6.3%	3.7%
2010s	15.7%	4.2%	10.4%

Source: Aswath Damodaran.

prudent behavior on behalf of the investor, but the results were far from consistent between the best and worst periods.

Housel's example provides yet another reason for long-term diversification. You just never know what the specific markets are going to do. If long-term returns were predictable, there wouldn't be any risk. It would be called making money, not investing. You have no control over when you were born or how the markets will perform over your investing lifetime. There is actually more luck involved in the process than many care to acknowledge or believe. Some will be blessed with enormous bull markets when they need it most. Others will have to deal with punishing bear markets at the most inopportune times. It doesn't seem fair but that's how it goes. This is why you never want to be stuck in just one market over the long term. If your personal long-term happens to be mistimed, you could be out of luck. There is always going to be the chance that you are invested in a poor performing asset class, geography, factor tilt, or strategy if you choose just one. Diversifying among and within all of these investment classes is one of the best ways to decrease the odds of having it severely impact your portfolio.

Let's take a look at a couple of examples to see the power of diversification in practice. Table 7.3 shows the annual returns by decade for both stocks and bonds. Even over decade-long periods, boring old bonds can outpace stocks, as we showed earlier. Stocks go through periods—like the 1950s, 1980s, and 1990s—of powerful returns where they seemingly can do no wrong. On the other hand, there are also times when they go nowhere for long stretches, like

Table 7.4   Annual Returns by Decade

	U.S. Stocks	Foreign Stocks	50/50 Portfolio
1970s	5.9%	10.1%	7.6%
1980s	17.3%	22.8%	20.1%
1990s	18.1%	7.3%	12.8%
2000s	−1.0%	1.6%	0.2%
2010s	15.7%	8.6%	12.2%

Sources: Aswath Damodaran, MSCI.

the 1930s and 2000s. Notice how uneven the annual performance numbers are over the decades.

Now what if you were to do a simple 50/50 split between stocks and bonds over those same decades? The third column shows the range of returns is much narrower, but the outlier negative decades vanish. When stocks struggled, bonds picked up the slack and when bonds struggled, stocks were there to bring up the performance.

These are just the results for U.S. markets, but the U.S. stock markets make up only half of the global market cap of stocks. Because of a home bias and familiarity with U.S.-based companies, many investors ignore investing in foreign markets. At times this has paid off. Other times, investors have felt like a fool for having a home bias. Like the example above, sometimes it comes down to dumb luck. Unless you have the ability to pick and choose when it makes sense to invest in the United States and when it makes sense to invest overseas, diversifying between the two is the prudent move. Table 7.4 shows the performance by decade for the S&P 500 and the MSCI EAFE, an index made up of developed countries in Europe, Australia, and the Far East. Each market takes their turn in the spotlight, but the performance numbers are drastically different in certain decades. Now look at the last column that shows a simple 50/50 split between the two and see how much more stable the returns look in comparison.

Looking at the long-term numbers, some investors might make the assumption that one can just stick to U.S. stock markets and avoid investing globally. While this positioning could work out if you happen to live in another period of time like the 1990s, you set yourself up for the risk of concentration if there is another period like the

1970s or 2000s, where there is severe underperformance in the U.S. markets.

AQR Capital Management, the quantitative asset management firm headed by the venerable Cliff Asness, put out a research paper a couple of years ago extolling the virtues of diversifying across international stock markets. These were their findings (emphasis mine):

> International diversification might not protect you from terrible days, months, or even years, but over longer horizons (which should be more important to investors) where underlying economic growth matters more to returns than short-lived panics, it protects you quite well. Over the short term, global diversification can disappoint. Markets tend to crash at the same time and as a result, globally diversified portfolios are more negatively skewed. Critics argue that international diversification offers little protection vs. purely domestic portfolios and can in fact be more dangerous if investors rely upon their long-term reduced volatility.
>
> We argue that this critique misses the point. *While short-term common crashes can be painful, long-term returns are far more important to wealth creation and destruction.* We show that over the long term, markets do not have the same tendency to crash at the same time. This is not surprising as even though market panics can be important drivers of short-term returns, over the long- term, country specific economic performance dominates. *Diversification protects investors against the adverse effects of holding concentrated positions in countries with poor long-term economic performance.* Let us not diminish the benefits of this protection. In a nutshell, international diversification works on a portfolio. Ignoring it is quite simply imprudent.[6]

Assume for a minute that you are a Japanese investor in the late 1980s. All around the world people are predicting that one day Japan will overtake the United States as an economic power. It wasn't out of the realm of possibilities in the eyes of many. Since the 1960s, you've experienced performance in excess of 20 percent per year in stocks, good enough to double your money every three and a half years. Why would you ever invest anywhere else? Take a look at the return comparison between U.S. stocks and those located in the Pacific region (mostly made up of Japanese companies) in the 1970s and 1980s:

	U.S. Stocks	Pacific Stocks
1970–1989	9.5%	20.5%

The Japanese property and stock market bubble was so great at the time that the property market in Japan was worth four times the entire U.S. real estate market by 1990, even though Japan is roughly the size of California. The stock market was trading near 100× earnings, when the long-term average for most markets is around 15×. Things got so out of hand in the Japanese bubble that there were more than 20 golf clubs that cost over $1 million to join.[7] To call Japan a bubble is almost an understatement. And just when you think things can't get any better, of course it all comes crashing down. You can imagine what followed over the next two and a half decades as the great bubble deflated:

	U.S. Stocks	Pacific Stocks
1990–2014	11.5%	1.4%

Having a home bias in your portfolio sets you up for the risk that you could see less than 2 percent returns for nearly two decades. Or you could double your money every three and a half years if you are lucky enough to invest in Japan in the 1970s and 1980s. Do you really want to risk a Japan-like scenario with your life savings? Global diversification will protect investors from the harm caused by a single country or region's economy or stock market. Interestingly enough, over the entire time horizon beginning in 1970, the two markets saw similar annual return streams, with the United States at 10.5 percent per year and the Pacific stocks at 9.4 percent per year. Obviously, timing can be everything when markets get completely out of whack with reality.

Everyone would like to know the perfect allocation mix between U.S. and foreign shares. Most advisors and investors will tell you to hold anywhere from 10 percent to 50 percent in international stocks. The truth is there's no right or wrong answer. The returns between the two asset classes should be fairly similar over longer time horizons if they follow similar paths as we've seen in the past. There will be differences over time from foreign currency fluctuations, but forecasting currencies is very difficult to do, as well. U.S. investors do spend down their portfolio in dollars, so an overweighting to U.S. stocks for retirees could be warranted. Longer time horizons are always situational. Maybe you'll get lucky by overweighting U.S. stocks over the next few decades. Maybe emerging markets continue to grow and develop their markets at a rapid rate and they're the big winners in the coming years. The best allocation will always be the one you're most comfortable with, which allows you to stick with it over time.

It's going to be impossible for a diversified portfolio to completely sidestep the pain when we experience periods like the great financial crisis from 2007 to 2009. Diversification isn't about the short term. It's about the long term. It requires patience, because building a diversified portfolio means that there are going to be times that pieces of your portfolio are going to drive you mad. Always remember that it's the performance of your entire portfolio that matters, not the individual parts.

But it's also worth pointing out that long term is context and situation dependent. It can mean different things to different people and organizations. You do have to spend the money you save and invest eventually, so there is the off chance that the markets are going to be uncooperative during the window you that you need to sell down your assets for living expenses, your kid's college fund, or any other reason. This is yet another reason that it's a prudent choice for investors to diversify. It allows you to take into account not only the risk in the markets, but also the risk in your personal circumstances, which include your varying time horizons.

Mean Reversion and Rebalancing

Complaining about the food served in county jails is a favorite pastimes for inmates. So it was somewhat shocking to a prison guard from a Midwestern country jail when he discovered that inmates sentenced to six months or so of jail time were gaining an average of 20 to 25 pounds over their stay behind bars. Once this was discovered, they searched for answers from a team of researchers. The inmates had access to the exercise yard so that wasn't the problem. When asked, none of them blamed the food, the accommodations, or the lack of exercise. The reason actually had more to do with the prison clothes, if you can believe it. The orange jumpsuits that serve as the uniform in prison are very baggy. They were so loose on the inmates that it was difficult for them to tell that they were slowly gaining weight because they didn't have their normal-fitting clothes to give them the signal that they were incrementally gaining weight. There was no safety net to let them know this was happening. Once they tried to fit back into their normal clothes following their jail time, they finally realized how much weight they had gained. Without clothes that fit to give them some sort of a measurement and benchmark to keep their weight in check, the inmates were adding pounds that went unnoticed.[8]

Think of rebalancing a portfolio in the same way. Rebalancing keeps your portfolio from getting overweight (see what I did there?) in any one investment or asset class. Rebalancing is the process of selling some of what has gone up in price and buying some of what has gone down in price to put your portfolio back in line with your stated asset allocation target weights. Just as asset allocation is worthless without diversification, diversification is worthless without rebalancing. These three pieces to the portfolio management process should be always and forever intertwined with one another.

Your first instinct when you see a volatile market will be to get as far away as possible. Most of the time, the opposite reaction will lead to far better results. Rebalancing into the volatility is actually the correct move the majority of the time (remember, there's no such thing as always or never in the markets). Volatility is actually a prerequisite for rebalancing and finding investment opportunities, especially in a broadly diversified portfolio that carries a wide range of investment classes. Whenever the markets make a big move in either direction or abruptly change course from gains to losses or vice versa, investors rush to make snap judgments to figure out why it happened. The simplest explanation is usually the correct one, and in most cases it's mean reversion. I'm sorry to ruin a good narrative, but it's true. No broad market rises in a straight line forever just like no asset class crashes for good either. Mean reversion contends that outperforming markets will eventually underperform while underperforming markets will eventually outperform. Mean reversion is conceptually simple to grasp, but harder to figure out in real time, as the average for most markets and valuation levels is probably a moving target and the timing of the reversion is always subject to change. But if you understood nothing more than the fact that the markets and the economy move in cycles you're better off than the majority of the investing public.

Studies on the timing of when to perform a systematic rebalance give varying results, but the main finding of a Vanguard study showed the act of rebalancing itself, no matter the interval (quarterly, semiannually, annually, etc.) was the key to investor success.[9] You're automating a contrarian approach in this way as you buy the relative losers and sell the relative winners. Everyone knows the phrase buy low, sell high, but most don't understand how to actually put it into practice. Rebalancing is a systematic approach of buying low and selling high, every time you do it. Some investors prefer a rebalance every time their asset allocation drifts away from the target weights. Others pick a specific date or time frame. Really, the best rebalancing technique will be the one that forces you to follow it over time. Many fund firms have an automatic rebalance feature that can make life easy for investors so you don't have to take any action. Automating good decisions like this takes the emotions out of the equation. If you can't or won't rebalance, setting a predetermined asset allocation does you no good. There will always be a great reason to *not* rebalance. Most of the good investment decisions you'll make over your lifetime will be the ones that feel like they're not right at the time.

Author and investor William Bernstein showed in a study that the diversification and rebalancing bonus is close to 0.5 percent annually,[10] but like the 90 percent asset allocation study, it's impossible to know what it will be in the future because of changing market conditions. There will be times when you can look back and see that rebalancing was the perfect move to make and other times when letting your portfolio drift would have led to better performance numbers. But this line of thinking misses the point. While rebalancing can provide a nice boost to performance, the biggest benefit of rebalancing comes from controlling risk, not enhancing returns. Risk management isn't something you can turn on and off when you feel like it. Take care of the risk and the performance should take care of itself. Eventually you can't help but see a performance boost from a disciplined rebalancing system through the behavioral benefits alone. Over time, fading the emotions of other investors will likely pay off.

Let's take a look at the rebalancing bonus in practice. These were the annual return numbers for the U.S., European, and Pacific stock markets from 1970 through late 2014:

European Stocks	10.5%
Pacific Stocks	9.5%
U.S. Stocks	10.4%

All three showed similar long-term returns over time. But if you were to combine the three markets into an equal-weighted portfolio allocation with an annual year-end rebalance back to the equal weights, the annual return of the portfolio jumps to 10.8 percent per year, higher than all three individually. How can this be, you might ask? It's because each market had years when they were the leaders and others when they were the laggards. Every single year this strategy would be selling the winners and buying the losers. In this case, risk management was the focal point, but returns were actually the beneficiary. Take care of the risk and the returns should take care of themselves.

There is a point of clarification that's needed here on mean reversion, though. Mean reversion has more to do with the broader markets, asset classes, risk factors, or investing styles, not necessarily individual stocks. For instance, Walmart produced a 40-year annual return of roughly 23 percent, good enough to turn $10,000 into over $39 million. Since the lows were hit in late 2002, Apple stock is up nearly 2,000 percent. On the other hand, as we saw in Chapter 5, almost half of all individual stocks suffered permanent declines of around 70 percent. There's no such thing as mean reversion in individual stocks. Companies go bankrupt. Others get bought out. Some go down but don't come back up while others are the proverbial lottery ticket stock.

Predicting risk is actually much easier than predicting returns. We know risk will be there. Over any decade-long period we can't be so sure the performance will necessarily be there. That's where patience and discipline come into play. Asset allocation is a slow game. It's never in a hurry. It doesn't work all the time but it works enough of the time to be effective.

Asset allocation is really emotional diversification as well as risk management. Adding together two asset classes with similar return expectations, such as U.S. and international stocks, makes sense because it reduces the volatility of your results, thus (hopefully) reducing the volatility of your reactions. There's not a perfect number of subasset classes and risk factors to include in a well-diversified portfolio. It depends on how difficult the ongoing maintenance and implementation becomes with each added fund or strategy. There's no need for three large-cap value funds in a single portfolio because you run the risk of overdiversification and the headaches that can come from having to track and keep up with too many different variables. The worst thing you can do for a good plan is strive for a perfect one. Going for a perfect plan by making continuous changes is much worse than implementing a solid plan that you stick with and utilize in a disciplined process.

Risk Factors, Value Investing, and the Power of Patience

Market participants are anything but rational. This is why markets can be and are beaten by many successful investors. But the number that can do this over longer time frames is very small, as we saw in Chapter 6.

While many would say that the fault rests completely on the shoulders of the portfolio managers and fund companies themselves for the underperformance, investors have to take some of the blame for this, as well. Chasing past performance is a time honored tradition of investors, both large and small. But there are active strategies that can diversify your portfolio—things like value, size, quality, momentum, dividend-paying stocks, and so on. These are all risk factors that come and go from the list of top performers, but if you can find an ETF or an actively managed fund that has a repeatable process (quantitative funds, smart beta and fundamental indexing all come to mind) then you'll have a better idea of the possibility of underperformance eventually exhibiting mean reversion. Unless you have superior knowledge of a different kind of active strategy, odds are that the first sign of underperformance for any extended period of time will cause problems because you can't lean on mean reversion from a good process.

How diversified you are as an investor depends on how willing you are to be different from the broader domestic and international total market funds. In finance-speak, you can run what is called a core-satellite approach and make adjustments depending on your tolerance for risk and being different than the market The core would be an S&P 500 index fund or a total stock or bond market fund. The satellites would be the different factor bets based on size (small or mid caps), quality (dividends or shareholder returns), asset class (REITs), geography (emerging markets, foreign developed markets) or risk factors (value, momentum). How far you stray from the core into the different satellites should be determined by how you handle your portfolio differing from the market's return. Diversification is important, but it should be balanced with your own ability to hang on and implement a portfolio strategy.

Any diversified portfolio is going to have leaders and laggards. That's true of a portfolio filled with active strategies or one filled entirely with index funds. Index funds and ETFs help in the sense that you know exactly what you're getting, even if that means sustaining periodic losses. But there is something to be said for the power of a simple portfolio. Researchers looked at the performance of the nation's largest pension plans from 1987 to 1999. The asset allocation for these plans was fairly similar across the board, close to a 60/40 split between stocks and bonds. Out of the 243 plans in the study, each investing hundreds of millions or even billions of dollars, 90 percent of them failed to beat a simple 60/40 portfolio made up of an S&P 500 index fund and the Lehman Brothers Aggregate Bond Index, two of the broadest market indexes available.[11] A simple portfolio is a good starting point. Any changes from there should be based on your appetite for risk and understanding of the different asset classes and risk factors.

The Value Premium

Psychologists have determined that the left hemisphere of our brain reacts to responses received on a consistent basis and tries to turn everything we're trying to comprehend into a story. This helps shape our beliefs into a narrative. They call this part of the brain the interpreter because it's always looking for ways to frame things in terms of cause and effect, even if it comes to the wrong conclusion.[12] Thinking this way can lead us astray as we assume what has happened in the past was clear to see and inevitable, but we fail to consider other outcomes.

The Significant Objects Project was a research effort undertaken by two authors, Rob Walker and Joshua Glenn. The experiment was designed to test the hypothesis that "narrative transforms the insignificant into the significant." What these researchers did was take 100 items of garage-sale quality that weren't worth much and try to dress them up with nothing more than a narrative by having volunteer writers craft fictional back-stories on each item to sell them on eBay. In total, the objects they bought cost less than $130. But once these inexpensive items were paired with a good story behind them, they were able to net over $3,600 in sales on eBay! A good narrative transformed a simple shot glass into a $76 sale. An oven mitt went for $52. A jar of marbles was sold for $50. This is how powerful stories can be on our perception of value. We prefer emotional stories to accurate data.[13]

The problem with narratives is that they often fail as investment ideas. This is because those ideas are usually baked into the price of whatever stock or market that narrative is being based on. The value premium is an anomaly that's partly based on the use of narratives. Historically speaking, value stocks have outperformed the rest of the market by anywhere from 2 to 5 percent, depending on the time frame and markets involved. In simplistic terms, value investing is buying cheap assets that are either underappreciated by the market or have become beaten down in price. Value stocks are shares of those companies that trade for lower multiples based on company measures such as book value, earnings, or cash flows.

There are two theories that try to explain why the value-investing anomaly exists: (1) Investors prefer a narrative when buying stocks, so sexy growth stories and glamour stocks tend to receive the most attention from investors and the media. Most people assume great companies should make for great stocks, without considering valuation. Fast-growing stocks have new products that are well-known by the public. Many have recognizable CEOs or founders as the face of the company. Time after time investors overestimate the future prospects of expensive stocks in the growth stage. This leaves the cheaper stocks overlooked. Beaten down stocks are beaten down for a reason, so it's difficult for investors to talk themselves into investing in cheap shares because there will usually be bad news surrounding value stocks. (2) Academic literature says that investors should earn higher returns for accepting higher levels of risk. Value stocks can become distressed businesses, which make their future results seem more uncertain as well as creating more volatility in the stock price. In essence, higher reward for higher risk taken.

Each of these theories plays a role in the historical value premium. Another, much simpler explanation is that buying value works over the long term because it doesn't always work all the time. For example, during the buildup of the tech bubble in the mid to late 1990s, growth stocks outperformed their value counterparts by more than 10 percent per year for six years running. That's a difference most investors cannot ignore. Yet once the tide turned, value stocks went on to outperform growth over the following 14 years by over 5 percent a year, completely reversing the previous trend. Over the entire 20-year period covered, from 1994 to 2013, value stocks outperformed growth stocks by almost 1.5 percent per year.[14] Only very patient investors were able to experience this outperformance. Others got sucked into the narrative of the transformative technology of the Internet age and got burned once the bubble burst. So value investing works . . . eventually.

Over the long term can be a very subjective phrase that's completely context dependent to each investor's particular circumstances. You might have to be very patient to get to the point where the long term finally comes into play. If you choose to invest in value stock funds, you have to be patient. It works over time, but not all the time.

The Rise of Smart Beta

Smart-beta strategies are a systematic way to construct a fund by using a risk factor or combination of risk factors to alter a market index. It's a process of weighting the companies in an index differently or screening out certain types of companies that you would like to invest in. It's a way to distinguish a portfolio from the market by utilizing many of the benefits of index fund investing (systematic, low cost, low turnover, tax efficient) without perfectly mimicking the actual index. Smart-beta strategies usually focus on a specific risk factor or combination of factors such as value stocks, small- or mid-cap stocks, momentum stocks, high-quality stocks, and periodically rebalancing the strategy using a rules-based process. Most indexes are cap-weighted, meaning the holdings are weighted by the size of the market cap. Apple is one of the largest publicly traded stocks in the world by market cap, so the stock would have a correspondingly large weight in the S&P 500. A much smaller company would have a smaller weighting.

Many of these strategies are called indexes, but really they are quantitative investment strategies. Remember, there is nothing special about index funds. The biggest advantage they have over the majority of active mutual funds is the fact that they are disciplined. This is why smart-beta funds should have staying power. They take the behavioral element out of the equation. Smart beta—or fundamental indexing, factor investing, strategic beta or whatever marketing names they will come up with in the future—is going to continue to gain market share. It will become cheaper and Wall Street will come up with many more ways to package different strategies and risk factors. I think these strategies can make sense as part of a broadly diversified portfolio if you know what you're getting yourself into. How much to put into each depends on a number of factors:

1. How different do you want to be from the market? To earn higher returns than the market you have to be willing to accept different returns than the market at times. Sometimes better, sometimes worse. There was a period in the 1980s and 1990s where small-cap value stocks underperformed the market for 18 years. Eventually they paid off, but that's a long time for investors to wait. Patience is a prerequisite for these strategies.
2. Can you stomach the possibility of higher risks to earn higher expected returns? Capitulation is perhaps the biggest risk for investors in these strategies. If you're going to invest in them, stay in them for the long haul. Don't get scared out because they're not working at the moment. Expectations are important. You never want to get to the point where you are surprised by a period of over- or underperformance.
3. Are you willing to rebalance and continue to put money into strategies that are down? This is really the only way smart beta strategies can work over time. You have to be willing to systematically buy low and sell high, otherwise they lose their long-term benefits.
4. The cost of owning the entire market is basically free or a rounding error using basic index funds. Factor strategies are much cheaper than index-hugging, active mutual funds, but expect to pay more for them than a basic total market index fund.

It's also possible that the premiums for these strategies will fall in the future for the simple fact that they are more widely known through academic research and the availability to invest in them through ETFs and mutual funds. In the past it would have been very difficult to put together these types of funds in a cost-efficient manner for the average investor. Now ETFs make them available to everyone at a fraction of the cost you would have paid in the past. This is a great thing for investors, but it drives up the competition. It's possible that these risk premiums will narrow in the future. A more likely outcome is that they will become more volatile. The ease of access to these types of strategies will make it much easier for investors to pile in after they have a string of successes, and pile out after the inevitable periods of underperformance. There will be more weak hands and they will be the ones that will run to the exits at the first sign of trouble. Jumping in and out and chasing past performance severely cuts down on any advantage a systematic strategy provides.

However, I'm skeptical that these premiums will ever go away permanently, for the simple fact that they don't work all the time. Our brains automatically and unconsciously expect a third repetition after we see two in a row of something. There have been studies that looked into the response of subjects trying to make forecasts about unpredictable events. Even though the subjects were told ahead of time that what they were looking at was unpredictable, they still thought that they could do it, even if everyone else would fail. This tells you all you need to know about the patience of some investors. Not everyone will be able to handle long-term strategies in the short term. There aren't enough steady hands with the required patience to see value strategies through the down cycles. You have to commit to these types of strategies, not use them when they feel comfortable. The reason certain strategies work over the long term is because sometimes they don't work over the short to intermediate term. One of my common sense rules of thumb states that as the expected returns and volatility of an investment increase, so too does poor behavior. It becomes more tempting to try to time the up and down cycles in these strategies. The riskier the investment the riskier the behavior tends to be. At times it will feel foolish to hold small caps or value stocks if large caps or growth stocks are outperforming (another reason to diversify). But it would be even more foolish to give up on a strategy that has merit just because it isn't working right now.

Table 7.5   The Value and Size Premiums

	Large-Cap	Large-Cap Value	Small-Cap	Small-Cap Value
1930s	–0.10%	–5.70%	2.30%	–2.60%
1940s	9.20%	12.70%	14.90%	19.80%
1950s	19.40%	18.40%	19.20%	19.60%
1960s	7.80%	9.40%	13.00%	14.40%
1970s	5.90%	12.90%	9.20%	14.40%
1980s	17.50%	20.60%	16.80%	20.10%
1990s	18.20%	16.80%	15.50%	16.20%
2000s	–0.90%	4.10%	9.00%	12.80%
1930–2013	9.70%	11.20%	12.70%	14.40%

Source: Dimensional Fund Advisors.

You also have to understand what you're buying. Not all value strategies are the same. Computers can't replicate Warren Buffett's success, so you have to set reasonable expectations. Buying undervalued assets is the entire point of investing so even if it doesn't work all the time, over longer time periods it should work most of the time, which again, is all you can ask for as an investor.

But the biggest issue with active funds or even factor-based funds has nothing to do with investment strategy and everything to do with investor behavior. There is one emotion that trumps nearly everything when it comes to selecting and sticking with any strategy over time—doubt. Some of the best historical risk premiums could actually underperform the broader market for over a decade.

See Table 7.5 for the long-term outperformance figures for small caps and value stocks going all the way back to the 1930s. Both small and value have outperformed the market historically, but there's a catch. You have to be very patient as an investor for this to work out. From 1983 to 2010, just about 27 years, large caps outperformed small caps. The same thing occurred from 1946 to 1966 and again from 1969 to 1978. That's a collective 56 years of underperformance dating back to 1926. This means much of that small-cap premium comes in heavy doses and doesn't last long. Small-cap value underperformed the market for 18 years in the 1980s and 1990s. In the 1950s and 1960s small-cap value underperformed the S&P 500 for another 15 years and it happened again from 1969 to 1976. Dating back to 1927, that's a collective 40 years of underperformance covering three distinct periods of time.[15]

Small-cap stocks are simply those that have small market caps, normally defined as those companies that are below $2 billion in market cap (mid caps would be around $2 to $10 billion and large caps over $10 billion). In many ways the small-cap premiums make sense in theory. Smaller companies have more room to grow. They're not as mature as large-cap companies. Research analysts mostly shun small-caps because the larger institutional clients can't buy many of the small-cap names since they don't move the needle (another advantage the average investor has over the pros). Small caps are less liquid so it's harder to trade in and out of them with larger pools of capital. Many small-cap stocks don't make it because they fail, but the high quality companies that do make it earn very good returns.[16]

There are some caveats to these historical return figures. It's worth noting that it was nearly impossible to put together a legitimate portfolio of small-cap value stocks before the 1980s without incurring huge costs for commissions, as well as market impact costs, because of their liquidity constraints. So don't necessarily take these numbers as hard and fast rules. There are legitimate theoretical and behavioral reasons to assume that the small-cap and value premiums will continue in the future, but I would caution investors to temper their expectations.

Doubt causes investors to abandon a strategy after it's down. Intelligent investors who understand the strategies and factors they invest in will be systematically buying underperforming asset classes and risk factors, assuming they are a staple in their portfolio, by fading fear and greed over and over again. It won't always work out perfectly, but you're not shooting for perfection, just reasonable results to grow your wealth.

Every investor needs to ask themselves an important question before putting together an asset allocation plan: What's my breaking point that will cause me to capitulate and sell? It could be an investment that contains risk you don't appreciate or understand. It could be large drawdowns. It could be as simple as being different from the market year in and year out. Figuring out that capitulation point is going to be the glue that holds your strategy together, regardless of how many different asset classes, funds, or strategies you employ.

When I said that every position, fund, or asset class in your portfolio should serve a purpose, I didn't just mean that from the perspective of diversification and lowering your risk. I meant it from a behavioral perspective as well. Since there's no magical asset allocation to each and every asset class, you have to strike the right balance between sleeping well at night and reaching your long-term goals. The right asset allocation gives you the best chance of staying out of harm's way by making a huge mistake when one piece of your portfolio is lagging the other parts. You'll always hate something in your portfolio. Just make sure you can live with that hate and understand why it's happening. That will hopefully give you the intestinal fortitude to not only hang on through the underperformance, but also add to it over time from your investments that are performing well. Sell high and buy low sounds easy from afar, but is very difficult to pull off under actual market conditions.

In the future it will be easier than ever to invest in different risk factors and combinations of risk factors. My advice is to only invest in those areas that you understand. You have to be comfortable with the risk profiles and diversification benefits when using factor-based strategies on their own or combined together.

How to See It Through

Your investment plan should be designed specifically for the end user—you. Don't build the one you think you should; build the one you know you will follow. You have to be brutally honest with yourself about your ability to handle risk. Most portfolios will be similar in many ways but the implementation will be very different.

This is difficult for some investors to hear, but it's not your plan that's going to fail. It's your ability to implement the plan that will likely be the culprit. Usually this happens at an inflection point, either after a crash or after large market gains. That's when it's going to be easy to lose your head. Too much or too little risk in a portfolio can cause huge emotional swings during these periods. Capitulation is never a place you want to find yourself.

Also remember—nothing is permanent until you make it so. You don't have to play the binary all-in or all-out game when building a portfolio. You can make minor changes along the way if you've determined after the course of a cycle of fear and greed that you don't have the right asset allocation in place. Life happens and a risk tolerance can and will change. Just don't make these decisions lightly and at the extremes in sentiment. While it's important to understand market and economic cycles, it's even more important to understand your personal financial lifecycle. There are huge differences between the needs of an investor who is closing in on retirement and one who is just starting out in the workforce. Former Fed Chairman Ben Bernanke once said, "Life is amazingly unpredictable; any 22-year-old who thinks he or she knows where they will be in 10 years, much less in 30, is simply lacking imagination." Keep this in mind when making comparisons to other investors.

No one knows exactly how their life is going to turn out. From small portfolio to big, saving to spending, growth to preservation and all of the stages in-between, your investment portfolio will change and evolve with you, as well. Remember the whole goal is to match your future needs, dreams, desires, and objectives—your future liabilities—with the current assets in your portfolio. This can get lost in the day-to-day market noise.

Over decade-long time horizons, your investment performance will mainly be derived from how you handle corrections, bear markets, and market crashes. During every single bear market there will be times when you wonder if the losses will ever stop. You will always wonder how much lower the market can go. The economic news will be terrible. Other investors around you will be depressed. Pessimism becomes pervasive.

Technology is going to continue to make is easier than ever to build a broadly diversified portfolio. Costs will be close to zero for portfolio management in the future. It's the implementation and ongoing maintenance that will separate the winners from the losers. Having the discipline to stick with a good plan even when it doesn't feel right is an underappreciated skillset.

The point is not to predict every bear market or crash, but to psychologically prepare for them ahead of time. Knowing this event can and will occur is half the battle because you will set up your investment plan to take it into consideration. The long term is inclusive of market losses. Prepare yourself and act accordingly. Unfortunately, investing in risky assets involves the risk of losing boatloads of money from time to time. If you want the safety of cash or short-term bonds, then be prepared to earn much lower returns.

You should notice a clear pattern in the asset class performance in Table 7.6.[17] While the real (after inflation) returns are not all exactly the same across the various countries, in each case the long-term returns in stocks is much greater than bonds. There's no reason

Table 7.6   Real Returns by Country

Country	Stocks	Bonds
Australia	7.4	1.5
Canada	5.7	2.1
Denmark	5.2	3.1
Finland	5.3	0.0
France	3.2	0.0
Germany	3.2	−1.6
Ireland	4.1	1.4
Italy	1.9	−1.5
Japan	4.1	−1.0
Netherlands	4.9	1.5
New Zealand	6.0	2.0
Norway	4.3	1.8
Portugal	3.7	0.6
South Africa	7.4	1.8
Spain	3.6	1.4
Sweden	5.8	2.6
Switzerland	4.4	2.2
United Kingdom	5.3	1.4
United States	6.6	1.9
World	5.2	1.8

Source: Credit Suisse.

to assume that stocks shouldn't continue to offer a risk premium over bonds in the future because stocks are simply riskier than bonds. If that doesn't happen consistently then we have bigger problems on our hands than your portfolio. Of course, there will always be short to intermediate periods of time when stocks will underperform bonds in certain countries. Manias and panics will always be part and parcel of the financial markets as long as humans are making investment decisions. The booms and busts will occasionally alter this long-term relationship in the short term. In the words of Kurt Vonnegut, "So it goes."

Globalization is making the world a flatter place, as technology is slowly leveling the playing field and allowing people from all walks of life to have access to insane amounts of information. There are also sure to be upheavals and crises in different countries and regions around the globe. Increased globalization will, at times, result in spill-over effects into the rest of the world. Other times, crises will be contained in certain areas that don't have diversified economies or markets. The United States has been one of the clear winners of the past century in terms of becoming an economic powerhouse and providing investors with juicy returns in risk assets. While the United States has many built-in advantages, remember, that America was once an emerging market too. From the late 1700s to the early 1900s, the United States averaged a recession every two years.[18] Owning risky assets such as stocks can be thought of as a way to ride the coattails of intelligent people as they continue to innovate. It has never paid to bet against human ingenuity. Investing in foreign markets is a bet that people in other parts of the world wake up every morning wanting to improve their standing in life as well.

Many assume that globalization should lead to more integrated markets and higher correlations in investment returns. While there will be times when it will feel like you should only own a single market (most likely this will make sense after the fact), diversification will continue to act as a prudent risk control for investors. No two markets are ever the same and there are far too many dynamics at work which will cause disruption and differences going forward no matter how far globalization spreads. With expected returns to stocks being fairly similar across the different countries, it makes little sense to try to pick and choose exactly which single market represents the best opportunity in the future. Diversification is the antidote for a cloudy crystal ball about the future winners. Global diversification offers diversification of individual securities, economies, valuations, bubbles, and crashes.

Asset allocation is the nerve center of the portfolio. It's an important decision that will determine your expected risks and returns. But it's far more important that you're able to stick with the allocation that you choose as opposed to picking the most optimized version according to the text books.

Key Takeaways from Chapter 7

- Asset allocation will never garner headlines, but it is by far the most important portfolio decision you will make. Stock picking is for home-run hitters who will likely strikeout. Asset allocation is for those who wish to safely get on base time after time with a high probability for success.
- Diversification is the willingness to admit you don't know what's going to happen in the future. Asset allocation does not

work without diversification, which does not work without a disciplined rebalancing process.

- Think globally with your portfolio because no one knows where the best and worst performing asset classes will come from in the future.

Notes

1. Tim Ferriss, *The 4-Hour Workweek: Escape 9–5, Live Anywhere, and Join the New Rich* (New York: Crown, 2009).
2. Roger G. Ibbotson and Paul D. Kaplan, "Does Asset Allocation Policy Explain 40, 90, or 100 Percent of Performance?" *Financial Analysts Journal*, 2000, https://corporate.morningstar.com/ib/documents/MethodologyDocuments/IBBAssociates/AssetAllocation Explain.pdf.
3. Robert Zemeckis, *Back to the Future II*, Movie, Amblin Entertainment, 1989.
4. Howard Marks, *The Most Important Thing Illuminated: Uncommon Sense for the Thoughtful Investor* (New York: Columbia University Press, 2013).
5. Morgan Housel, "The Hard Truth: Successful Investing Involves a Lot of Luck," *Motley Fool*, July 29, 2014, www.fool.com/investing/general/2014/07/29/investing-luck.aspx.
6. Clifford S. Asness, Roni Israelov, and John M Liew, "International Diversification Works (Eventually)," AQR Capital Management, March 3, 2010, http://papers.ssrn.com/sol3/papers.cfm?abstract_id=1564186.
7. Edward Chancellor, *Devil Take the Hindmost: A History of Financial Speculation* (New York: Plume, 2000).
8. Brian Wassink, *Mindless Eating: Why We Eat More Than We Think* (New York, Bantam, 2007).
9. Frank Kinniry, "The Rebalancing Act: Coaching Clients to Stay Focused," Vanguard Research, June 3, 2014, https://advisors.vanguard.com/VGApp/iip/site/advisor/researchcommentary/article/IWE_Inv ComRebalancingAct.
10. William Bernstein, "The Rebalancing Bonus: Theory and Practice," Efficient Frontier, 1996, www.efficientfrontier.com/ef/996/rebal.htm.
11. William Bernstein, *The Four Pillars of Investing: Lessons for Building a Winning Portfolio* (New York: McGraw-Hill, 2010).
12. Michael Mauboussin, *The Success Equation: Untangling Skill and Luck in Business* (Boston: Harvard Business School Publishing, 2012).
13. Dan Ariely, "The Significant Objects Project," DanAriely.com, December 2009, http://danariely.com/2009/12/25/the-significant-objects -project/.

14. Ben Carlson, "Q & A with Alpha Architect's Wes Gray: Part 1," *A Wealth of Common Sense,* http://awealthofcommonsense.com/qa-alpha -architects-wes-gray-part/.

15. Fama French database, available at http://mba.tuck.dartmouth .edu/pages/faculty/ken.french/data_library.html.

16. Paul Merriman, "8 Lessons from 80 Years of Market History," MarketWatch, December 29, 2014, www.marketwatch.com/story/8 -lessons-from-80-years-of-market-history-2014-11-19.

17. Elroy Dimson and Mike Staunton, Credit Suisse Global Investment Returns Yearbook 2014, *Credit Suisse Research Institute, February 2014,* http://gallery.mailchimp.com/6750faf5c6091bc898da15 4ff/files/ global_investment_returns_yearbook_2014.pdf.

18. The National Bureau of Economic Research. www.nber.org.

CHAPTER

8

A Comprehensive Investment Plan

Have a plan. Follow the plan, and you'll be surprised how
successful you can be. Most people don't have a plan. That's why
it's easy to beat most folks.

—Bear Bryant

Nick Saban, the head football coach for the Alabama Crimson Tide, abides by a strict routine that he calls the *process*. Many credit this process for the success Saban has enjoyed in college football over the past couple of decades, including four BCS National Championships (and counting), one at LSU, and three at Alabama. Saban's process focuses only on those things that are within your control.

One of the major themes within the process is focusing on the big-ticket decisions that make a difference and systematically minimizing distractions everywhere else. Every day at noon, Saban eats the same exact lunch—a salad with lettuce, cherry tomatoes, and turkey slices served in a Styrofoam container. Automating his lunch decision allows Saban to focus on more important tasks at hand. That minor decision is eliminated.[1] Saban says that if you can "Eliminate the clutter and all the things that are going on outside and focus on the things that you can control with how you sort of go about and take care of your business. That's something that's ongoing, and it can never change."[2]

Saban doesn't spend his time focusing on implementing the latest and greatest offensive and defensive schemes. Instead it's about implementing the ones that are in place and executing. He asks his

149

players to focus on their effort, not the results of the last play or even the overall ball game. The thought process is that if the effort and discipline are there, the results will surely follow. He actually deemphasizes a focus on winning, because he knows the process will eventually pay off.[3] He preaches to his players that they need to play without emotion and be disciplined enough to take care of their job. Obviously, Saban's results speak for themselves. His maniacal focus on process has led to extraordinary outcomes, even though the outcomes haven't been the main focus of his message.

There are many parallels of Saban's approach to building an investment plan. No one controls short-term outcomes in the market and it's basically worthless to worry about them, yet this is what investors are constantly obsessing over. Automating good decisions is essential to investment success. As we discussed earlier, willpower has a shelf life. You need to let it rest just like any other muscle in the body. You can't spend all of your time worrying about making trivial decisions when it comes to your portfolio. The minutiae will eat you alive and can only lead to mistakes. In sports they say you can't control your talent, but you can control your effort. In the investing world, you can't control the markets, but you can control your emotions. It's also refreshing to see that Saban isn't concerned with new strategies for offensive and defensive game plans, but instead focuses on improving the ones currently in place. Investors who are constantly jumping from strategy to strategy could learn from this mindset. Eventually it's not about strategy, but implementation.

This focus on process over outcomes may seem trivial to some, but it's one of the most important distinctions you can make in portfolio management. Developing the proper process takes away the need to set specific goals because you will always be looking to improve and make better decisions. And a portfolio is a process, not just a one-time decision. It's going to constantly evolve as your life evolves. That doesn't mean it should change all the time, but that the process is ongoing. This is why, to bring it all together, investors need a comprehensive investment plan. None of it matters—philosophy, asset allocation, diversification, strategy—without a coherent plan.

Why Do You Need a Plan?

Stay the course and stick with your plan no matter what. These are great pieces of advice that are offered up to investors by financial advisors, investment books, and in the financial press. It's good advice. But so are the tried and true dieting maxims of eat less and work out more. Everyone knows what you *should* do, but *how* do you do it? How do you change your behavior?

For investors it all comes down to creating a comprehensive investment plan. Your plan should include everything we've talked about up to this point: your investment philosophy, asset allocation, a rebalancing schedule, what kinds of investments you will or won't make, and so on. This may seem like a minor distinction, but there is a huge difference between a portfolio and an investment plan. A portfolio is just a mix of different holdings. A plan allows you to utilize a portfolio to control your behavior to achieve your financial objectives.

One of the most underestimated risks for investors does not stem from volatility or market losses, but from not having a plan in place. Investors should always avoid situations where they don't know what they're doing. Even with a well-defined investment policy statement, there's really no way to guarantee with 100 percent certainty that your portfolio will be as successful as you would like it to be. But there is a sure way to fail—never implement a plan in the first place. In fact, if you don't have an investment plan in place that means you're speculating, not investing.

The only true guarantee we have in the markets is that things will go wrong and people's perception of risk will be in a constant state of change. Risk is actually more predictable than returns. A solid plan takes into account what could go wrong upfront, before disaster strikes, not after the fact. Contingencies should be planned for. Mapping out if/then statements for a number of different scenarios makes for more favorable reactions during times of stress. It's never going to be easy, but having a plan in place reduces the burden of market losses. The point is, the markets should never surprise you. Since successful investing comes down more to your reactions than your actions, preparing yourself for anything is the best form of planning.

It can be confusing, but you're not always going to get reassurance from the markets. They don't always cooperate. Sometimes they agree with your stance. Other times, nothing is going to work. Try to focus your energy on how sound your decisions are, not necessarily the outcomes each and every time. Outcomes over shorter time frames can be nearly impossible to distinguish between good and bad, since luck plays a bigger role than most care to admit. The best process will only measure outcomes over the long term. You can't expect to make the perfect decision every single time. But making it most of the time and avoiding the worst decision will help. Think of it like losing weight. Working out and dieting for a week might not lead to the desired outcomes. But working out and eating a healthy diet over a number of years will. It's the repetition of good decisions that leads to favorable outcomes over time. Good investors have a high tolerance for repetition, even when it requires doing nothing over and over again.

It has to be an open-ended process as well. Goals are important but you have to be flexible. Studies shows that getting exactly what you planned for is basically a non-event for your brain activity. You would think that seeing the fruits of your labor should be satisfying. It should motivate people to continue on the path that they're on. Unfortunately, it doesn't do much for our feelings if we are already planning on something. We need a bigger hit of adrenaline or dopamine to get a bigger fix every time for the same emotional response. This can cause people to increase their risk and use forms of speculation to get that response.[4]

It's impossible to plan for every potential outcome. Not only are the markets in a continuous state of flux, but our lives are sometimes just as messy as the markets. There's no way you can know exactly how much money you're going to make throughout your career when you are just starting out. You can't plan on earning steady returns over time. No one knows when the next bear market or huge crash will occur. Sometimes you get lucky and your timing is perfect. Other times, through no fault of your own, the markets don't cooperate.

Setting up a systematic process imposes discipline on your lesser self. You will still have to make discretionary decisions many times over the years, but just know that you are by far the easiest person to fool. Understand why you should or shouldn't do something based on your knowledge of yourself and use a plan to create a hurdle that makes it difficult to make poor decisions.

The Investment Policy Statement (IPS)

The investment policy statement (IPS) is a written document that outlines how you would like to implement your portfolio and maintain it over time. Since portfolio management is an ongoing process, the IPS is the guidebook that will get you from point A to point B. The

IPS is where you write down all of your dos and don'ts, your if/then statements, and your goals and objectives. It's your plan of attack that guides your actions. The goal of the IPS is to keep you out of trouble and on the right path over time. The process of writing it down is important. It can be as little as a single page or it can fill a three-ring binder. It all depends on how many constraints and rules you need to place on yourself. It's your own personal checklist. Here are a few questions to consider when coming up with your personal IPS:

> What future liabilities, dreams, and desires will this money provide in the future?
> What are my expectations for this portfolio in terms of risk and returns?
> How much pain (read: losses) can I physically and financially handle?
> When will I buy and sell? What will trigger those decisions?
> What's my target asset allocation and when will I rebalance?
> What's my risk profile and time horizon for each investment or asset class within the portfolio?
> What's on my list of products, securities, or investment strategies that I will never invest in?
> How complex am I willing to make my portfolio?
> How much short-term liquidity will I require for emergencies and day-to-day spending?
> When will I make changes to my portfolio and plan over time?
> How will I maintain, implement, and review my IPS over time?
> How will I judge the success of my IPS?

At least annually, you'll want to review your personal IPS to make any corrections to your plan and maintain your portfolio. Some points of emphasis for the annual review:

> Am I saving enough? How much more do I need to save to hit my goals?
> Have my circumstances changed enough to warrant a change to my plan or portfolio?
> Has my willingness, ability, or need to take risk changed?
> How was my investment performance?
> How did I behave last year?
> What were my biggest mistakes or regrets?

There's a strange dichotomy in the investment process in that no one knows how the future will play out, but you still have to plan for the future by making educated approximations about how things will play out in the coming years and decades. The most important thing to remember is that your process should not be contingent on predicting the magnitude of future interest rate moves or the change in the stock market over shorter periods of time. Those things are out of your control and even the most seasoned investors are just guessing when they make predictions on those types of moves. Even Warren Buffett himself thinks that short-term forecasts are worthless. He stated that "We have long felt that the only value of stock forecasters is to make fortune-tellers look good. Even now, Charlie [Munger] and I continue to believe that short-term market forecasts are poison and should be kept locked up in a safe place, away from children and also from grown-ups who behave in the market like children."

Always err on the conservative side when setting return expectations. This should lead to a higher savings rate, which is never a bad thing. This gives you a personal margin of safety in case things go wrong. With low expectations, you can only be surprised on the upside. Depending on your actual performance and rate of savings, you can make adjustments as needed in your annual review.

The most important aspect of any IPS is to focus on those areas that are within your control and that you understand. Don't bother stressing about things that are out of your control or comfort zone. They are the proverbial crying over spilled milk. There's no reason to add additional stresses to your life.

Lifecycle Investing

On which end of your investing lifetime do you want your insecurity, so that you can have security at the other end?

—Nick Murray

The infamous 1979 *Businessweek* cover story entitled "The Death of Equities" is widely viewed as one of the best contrarian indicators of all-time. After the story ran, stocks went on to have one of the greatest bull markets in history over the ensuing two decades. After the constant volatility, sky-high inflation, and poor returns of the late 1960s and 1970s, investors were having a difficult time coming up with reasons to stay invested in stocks. This was even more pervasive in the younger demographic:

> Younger investors, in particular, are avoiding stocks. Between 1970 and 1975, the number of investors declined in every age group but one: individuals 65 and older. While the number of investors under 65 dropped by about 25 percent, the number of investors over 65 jumped by more than 30 percent. Only the elderly who have not understood the changes in the nation's financial markets, or who are unable to adjust to them, are sticking with stocks.[5]

The author of this piece is almost mocking the older crowd for staying with stocks, something that turned out to be a very wise move on their part. There's always something to be said for experience in the markets. A similar phenomenon took place following the Great Recession from 2007 to 2009. Recent events are fresh in young people's minds and they've seen their parent's retirement accounts take a beating along with any savings they have at this stage in their lives. The younger generation began to assume the worst from financial markets. A UBS Investor Watch survey on the financial habits of Millennials written a few years after the crisis looks eerily similar to the "Death of Equities" piece from the previous generation:

> The Next Gen investor is markedly conservative, more like the WWII generation who came of age during the Great Depression and are in retirement. This translates into their attitude toward the market as we see Millennials, including those with higher net worth, holding significantly more cash than any other generation. And while optimistic about their abilities to achieve goals and their financial futures, Millennials seem somewhat skeptical about long-term investing as the way to get there.[6]

Julius Caesar once said, "Experience is the teacher of all things." It's unfortunate, but true that our experiences can shape our views of the markets. So while it makes perfect sense on paper that young investors should be taking oodles of risk with their investments, if you're young but can't take the heat, you may have to ease into a risky asset allocation. While not ideal from a textbook point of view, the real world can be messy. Just remember that the biggest risk may be not taking enough risk to allow your savings to compound over the many decades you have to invest. Young people just have to frame it in terms of giving themselves more options in the future instead of trying to picture what they'll be doing in a retirement that could be three to four decades away.

Instead of looking at where they are in their lifecycle and using that to determine their risk profile and time horizon, many default to using the most recent memory that stands out in their mind about the markets. Investors have a nasty habit of extrapolating the recent past indefinitely out into the future. In fact, studies show that economic growth can even have an impact on people's happiness, which can affect their perception of risk in financial assets. Researchers looked at data on life satisfaction and compared it to economic growth in a number of countries. They found that happiness is around six times more sensitive to negative economic growth than it is to positive GDP. This is another form of loss aversion, whereby losses sting more than gains feel good. Difficult environments can leave lasting impressions on our psyches. So not only is it likely that your investments will be down, but your unhappiness will be rising, a terrible combination for making rational decisions with your money.[7]

While it makes sense to view your entire portfolio in aggregate for asset allocation and performance monitoring purposes, you can also think about it in terms of multiple time horizons. A portfolio is really just a stream of assets that should allow you to meet your various future liabilities. At its most basic level, how, when, and why you want to spend your future savings is the most important factor in determining your investment plan. College? House down payment? Retirement? Charitable giving? Heirs? Thinking about the answers to these questions helps a great deal when selecting the correct portfolio allocation and asset classes. It's really a guess for longer-term goals, but thinking in these terms gets your mindset going in the right direction.

Lifecycle investing is all about the fact that most market scenarios will have different implications on different groups of investors depending on the length of time they have remaining in the financial markets. How mature your portfolio is in terms of current market value versus future savings will have a lot to do with how you structure your plan. If you still have many years to save and invest you should actually welcome market volatility and downturns. If you will be spending down your portfolio, volatility can be both painful and stressful. Young investors should pray for a huge market crash early in their career. It will allow them to buy stocks at much lower prices and thus, increase future returns and the compounding effects through higher dividend yields. Retired investors should pray for the opposite, a bull market early in retirement, because a stock market crash can cause serious damage to risky assets when there's no new savings going into a portfolio or the need to use some of that money for spending purposes. This is why retirees shouldn't have all of their money tied up in stocks. It's too risky for short-term capital.

When you're younger and just starting out in the workforce, your greatest asset is not your savings or retirement accounts, but your human capital or future earnings power. Those future earnings are where your future savings will come from. If you're saving on a regular basis, say a percentage of each paycheck, you have something of a natural rebalancing mechanism in place. You'll be buying more shares of stocks when prices are lower and less when they're higher. Young people also have much more time to recover from bear markets. In theory, these things are true, but in reality, losing money in your first bear market, no matter how small the balance is in your account, feels like a swift kick in the teeth. For this reason, it could be prudent for young people to slowly work their way up to a full weighting in stocks. While not ideal, it matters more that you stick to your plan than how big your allocation to equities is right off the bat. Most young investors should be able to handle market volatility, but don't have the required experience to have a calm demeanor. Having said that, an exclusive focus on downside protection by sitting in bonds or cash excludes you from participating in the enormous upside and compounding effects seen in the stock market over longer time horizons. The earlier you start saving and compounding your wealth, the less you are forced to save later in life, when it's more likely that you'll have greater responsibilities.

For retirees or those approaching retirement, the thought process has to be much different than the younger crowd. There has to be a balance between the short-term risks of the need for spending money and the longevity risk of outliving your money. This will be an ongoing issue as life expectancies continue to rise and people live longer from advances in healthcare. The options for those nearing retirement without enough savings are less than ideal—work longer, save more money, lower your standard of living, or a combination of the three. Even if you have saved enough, those savings have to last for another 20 to 30 years, on average. That's a long time for the corrosive effects of inflation to take hold of your purchasing power. One million dollars in 2014 has the same buying power as roughly $450,000 in 1985. So over 30 years, inflation ate up over half of the purchasing power if that money was stuffed under a mattress.

It can also be difficult to go from the mindset of wealth accumulation to wealth preservation. How you become wealthy is much different than how you stay wealthy. Older investors have less time to make up losses through future savings, compound interest, or the ability to wait for a market recovery. For those investors who are in or approaching retirement, a good rule of thumb is not to have money tied up in stocks that you'll need to use for spending purposes within four to five years. It's too much of a risk that stocks could take a hit right when you need to sell if you have an all-stock portfolio.

Beating the Market

Ask almost anyone how their portfolio is performing and you'll likely get a performance update from the past week, month, or maybe quarter, if you're lucky. And the returns are usually framed in terms of the market. "I'm keeping up with the market." "I wish I had more invested in the market instead of diversifying." "I'm getting smoked by the market this year." While it makes for interesting cocktail conversations, beating the market can't be your lone measure of success as an investor. For most professionals in the industry, beating the market is the only thing that matters. For the individual investor, the only thing that matters is that you're on track to achieve your desired goals in the future. Think of a benchmark as your own personal expectations. It helps keep overconfidence from ruining your future results.

If you are able to beat the market, that's great. Good for you. Just know that success is fleeting in the financial markets. No one wins all the time. Hubris is an expensive mindset when you let it puff up your ego. You cannot rely exclusively on beating the market to achieve your goals. It sets the bar too high and can lead to a misalignment of expectations. Count yourself lucky if you can achieve market-equaling results. Earning average returns actually means you're an above-average investor when compared to other market participants. Beating your peers is much easier than beating the S&P 500. It's less about beating the market and more about not beating yourself. Behavioral alpha comes from being above average, keeping stress and complexity to a minimum, efficiently running your portfolio, and eliminating unforced errors. Professional investors are constantly debating the Efficient Market Hypothesis. Individuals should keep their process efficient and not spend their time worrying about debating the merits of theories.

Focus on structuring a portfolio for long-term success, not short-term tactics. While short-term inefficiencies in the market can be arbitraged away very quickly, no one has successfully figured out a way to arbitrage long-term thinking. Patience is the ultimate equalizer in the markets between pros and Joes.

Time is one of the most misunderstood, yet important, concepts to understand about the investment process. Time doesn't guarantee you anything, but it increases your probability for success when you use it to your advantage. Many investors have learned the hard way that trying to beat the market over shorter time frames can be more trouble than it's worth. A singular mission to outperform often leads to underperformance. The same logic applies when trying to minimize losses. A sole focus on downside protection usually leads to the opportunity cost of no upside participation.

Saving Money

When you're young, healthy, and new to the workforce, it's going to be nearly impossible to think about planning ahead for life's future issues such as retirement. Most likely, thinking that far out into the future will mean very little to you. This is why younger investors need to think in terms of what that future wealth can bring them—specifically, freedom and flexibility. The greatest thing that money can buy is time to do whatever it is that makes you happy. If you're forced to work later in life doing something you don't love to do for a paycheck, that's not a fun scenario for a young person to consider. Instead of framing it as retirement, something most people associate with getting old, think about what a healthy nest egg can do for your lifestyle: Work wherever you want? Early retirement? Freedom from the 9 to 5 job? Whatever the most annoying part of your life is, use that as your motivation to save. If you hate your job, save enough money so you don't have to work for a boss that you don't like. If you want to travel the world, save enough to go wherever your heart desires. Think in terms of your future self—the more you save now the less you owe yourself down the line to have to play catch-up.

While the markets have been a compounding machine over the past century or so, it really doesn't matter what you invest in if you're not a diligent saver. The funds you choose don't matter nearly as much as allowing compound interest to work in your favor. In fact, the bulk of your portfolio growth in the first two decades of investing will come from how much money you save. Assuming a 7 percent annual return on your portfolio and a 12 percent savings rate as a percentage of your income, it would take nearly 20 years until your investment gains would start to overpower the increase in value you see from contributions to your account. Over three-plus decades, assuming historical rates of return, a 5 percent annual increase in savings would produce the equivalent of roughly 1.5 to 2.0 percent per year in annual investment gains. Professional portfolio fund managers would kill for those kinds of performance gains.[8]

Your circumstances will change many times over in life's natural progression. There will have to be updates and corrections along the way. Your portfolio will look different over the years as your salary, family situation, and risk profile change. Just make sure you're making changes to your investment plan because of your situation, not the market's latest moves. And always make saving money a priority.

Taxes and Asset Location

Most people hate thinking about taxes, but you have to consider the tax efficiency of your portfolio from the perspective of asset location for a well-rounded financial plan. Anyone starting out saving should have as much of their long-term capital as possible in tax-sheltered accounts. This is a no-brainer for those funds you won't need to touch for many decades on end. Not only do your investment gains, income, and fund distributions grow tax-free, but there are no headaches involved with tax prep and worrying about missing something when filing a tax return. You get upfront tax breaks in retirement accounts like the 401(k) or backloaded tax breaks—meaning no taxes paid on the eventual retirement distributions—in Roth IRAs. You could try to calculate your future tax rate to figure out the optimal mix between the two types of accounts. But since no one knows what the jokers in Washington D.C. are going to do as far as tax policy goes, it probably makes sense to use one of each as a savings vehicle to diversify your tax situation. It's always good to have options.

For those who also invest in taxable accounts, it's worth noting that there are varying tax implications depending on the asset class. Bonds, REITs, high dividend-paying stocks, and pretty much anything with regular income payments besides tax-free municipal bonds should go in tax-deferred retirement accounts because they are tax inefficient assets. In a taxable account you would be paying taxes on the income received, which would lower your after-tax returns. Stock index funds and ETFs are far more tax efficient, so if you're going to invest in taxable accounts, stocks make more sense there.

However you have your assets spread out among taxable or tax-deferred accounts, always remember to look at your situation from an overall portfolio level. The only way to make informed decisions is by aggregating all retirement funds, college savings accounts, and savings vehicles in one place. This allows you to determine how liquid you are, what your net worth is, what your overall performance numbers are, how diversified your portfolio is, and what your true asset allocation mix looks like.

Key Takeaways from Chapter 8

- The only benchmark that matters is achieving your personal goals, not beating the market.
- For many the biggest risk is running out of money, not losing money.
- Investment principles should stay the same over time, but your personal circumstances will play a large role in determining your investment stance and risk controls.

Notes

1. Lars Anderson, "Nick Saban and the Process," *Sports on Earth*, July 2014, www.sportsonearth.com/article/85531726/the-process-nick-saban-university-of-alabama-crimson-tide.
2. Greg Bishop, "Saban Is Keen to Explain Process," *New York Times*, January 5, 2013, http://thequad.blogs.nytimes.com/2013/01/05/saban-is-keen-to-explain-process/.

3. Jason Selk, "What Nick Saban Knows About Success," *Forbes*, September 12, 2012, www.forbes.com/sites/jasonselk/2012/09/12/what-nick-saban-knows-about-success/.

4. Jason Zweig, *Your Money and Your Brain: How the New Science of Neuroeconomics Can Help Make You Rich* (New York: Simon & Schuster, 2008).

5. BusinessWeek, "The Death of Equities," *BusinessWeek*, August 13, 1979, www.businessweek.com/stories/1979-08-13/the-death-of-equities businessweek-business-news-stock-market-and-financial-advice.

6. UBS, "Think You Know the Next Gen Investor? Think Again," *UBS Investor Watch*, First Quarter 2014, www.ubs.com/content/dam/Wealth ManagementAmericas/documents/investor-watch-1Q2014-report.pdf.

7. Tim Harford, "Why Are Recessions So Depressing?" *The Undercover Economist*, October 28, 2014, http://timharford.com/2014/10/why-are-recessions-so-depressing/.

8. Ben Carlson, "When Saving Trumps Investing," *A Wealth of Common Sense*, http://awealthofcommonsense.com/saving-trumps-investing/.

CHAPTER 9

Financial Professionals

Good advice rarely changes, while markets change constantly. The temptation to pander is almost irresistible. And while people need good advice, what they want is advice that sounds good.
—Jason Zweig

It was my first week on the job and it felt like a watered-down version of the conference room in the most memorable scene from the movie *Boiler Room*. You know, the one where Ben Affleck's hotshot character struts into the conference room full of trainees and gives his famous speech to a group of new stockbrokers, saying, "I am a millionaire. It's a weird thing to hear, right?" My situation wasn't quite so dramatic, but there was a room full of confident investment analysts biding their time, waiting for the head of the department to come in and give his monthly assessment of the team. There was a ton of competition within the firm, so while people made small talk, you could tell that they were silently sizing each other up. I was the lowly intern so I took my rightful place on the outskirts of a table. This was my first taste of life at a large financial firm and it was actually quite exciting for a 21-year-old looking to make his way in the business.

The job entailed performing research on individual stocks for a group of sell-side analysts. The reason they're called sell-side analysts is because the firm sold the research to their clients, mostly professional investors. These are the people who closely track a sector or industry group of companies and issue buy, sell, or hold recommendations based on their research. Each investment analyst had at least one to two junior research analysts working for them (there was a lot of analyzing going on) and each analyst covered in the range of 10 to 15 stocks, spread out by the different sectors and industries. In total, the firm probably covered upward of 200 to 250 individual stocks.

When the head of the department finally walked into the room you could see the look of concern on his face. He let out an audible sigh as he stood at the head of the table to give the latest update on the current recommendations in place for the firm. He started out by sharing the aggregate number of buy recommendations all the analysts had on the stocks they covered. There were plenty of buys in these stocks; well over half of the stocks covered. Next he moved onto the hold recommendations. Not quite as many holds, but still a decent amount. Finally, it came time to let everyone know how many sell calls they had on the stocks in their universe. He was not pleased when he yelled, "We have a *total* of three sell recommendations right now . . . in the *entire* firm! Three! Can someone please put a sell signal on a stock they don't like? Any stock will do!"

It took me a while to realize what was going on here to figure out that it wasn't unique to this particular firm. This is basically how most of the industry worked. The analysts received some of their most prized information to create their research reports from the meetings and conference calls they had with the CEOs and other executives within the companies they covered. Other departments within the organization also provided different services to the companies covered beyond creating research reports to sell to clients. Many of the companies the investment analysts were covering were also clients of the firm in some other capacity. Had they put a sell signal on the company's stock, the analysts risked angering company management, potentially disrupting the relationship and business dealings. No one ever admitted this fact, but it seemed to be an unspoken rule to not rock the boat.

When I started at this firm, I was sure that these people were the masters of the universe. Everyone was intelligent. They seemingly knew everything there was to know about these stocks. Everyone had the educational pedigree—MBAs and CFAs galore. I got sucked into believing they could do no wrong. These opinions were slowly turned on their head, starting with the meeting that outlined the three sell ratings.

While these analysts were all very smart people, many hailing from the top business schools and using the most sophisticated discounted cash flow models you can build, there were forces beyond their control that dictated their actions whether they were willing to admit it or not. I learned some important lessons from this experience. First and foremost, incentives are everything, both inside and outside of the world of finance. You can't always make decisions based on your intelligence or what you really think or feel if there are incentives or disincentives at play within the organization's culture. Often times there are circumstances at play that force you into making choices you otherwise would not have made. In any of life's endeavors, understanding the motivations and incentives of others is essential.

Second, even though these people were all very intelligent, so are thousands and thousands of other market participants who follow the markets. (Trust me, there are some dumb ones too, but for the most part, intelligence is not the problem; it's too much intelligence and not enough common sense.) If you haven't spent a lot of time in the finance industry or have a solid grasp of the markets, it's easy to come away extremely impressed by the first smart person you come across. You start to believe everything they say because they sound intelligent. Just remember that there will always be someone smarter than they are and that emotional intelligence counts for much more than IQ.

Third, opinions don't take you very far if they're not backed up with skin in the game. I found buy and sell recommendations are much easier to make if you don't have to back them up with actual invested capital. I can't blame these analysts, because that's the nature of the industry. But there's something to be said for the emotions that come into play when you have your cold, hard savings invested and not just paper trades or opinions. Being wrong is a much different feeling than losing money. Emotions tend to affect future decisions once you've felt the sting of losses.

Finally, independence is of the utmost importance when you are receiving financial advice. Not all analysts are compromised or bad people. Many offered useful research even though their recommendations weren't the greatest. It's a difficult balancing act to put out research reports on companies that could have other financing arrangements or consulting relationships with these banks and brokerages. Also, you have to be aware of the types of short-term-oriented clients these analysts were doing research for. It was always buy, sell, or hold; not risk, patience, or time horizon. No one is ever going to be completely conflict free when giving advice for compensation. But the financial professionals you want to work with or take advice from will be transparent from the start with what kind of conflicts or compensation you are dealing with as a client. Honesty can go a long way when building trust.

Vetting Your Sources of Financial Advice

There seem to be opinions at the extremes for financial professionals that help manage money for others. Either we trust them way too much and expect them to be our saviors, such as Bernie Madoff when people assumed he could do no wrong before his scam was rooted out. Or we assume that they're all crooks and scumbags who can never be trusted, such as Bernie Madoff after his scam was discovered. Any time there are extreme opinions, the truth usually lies somewhere in the middle. While there are many financial professionals out there who are just looking to make a buck at your expense, there are also good, honest people who would like to help you reach your goals and improve your finances. The old saying—trust, but verify—is a good compromise. But you do need to know what to watch out for when taking advice, either face to face or from members of the financial media.

What draws most people in when receiving financial advice is a sense of authority and confidence. The more certain someone is about their ability to predict the future, the more comfortable you're going to be taking that advice because it gives you that elusive illusion of control. Since the markets seem so very easy in hindsight, they'll seem even easier if someone can only tell you exactly what's going to happen next. The conundrum is that no one knows what's going to happen in the future. Anyone giving you advice that tells you they know exactly what's going to happen next is either a charlatan or a liar. The higher the conviction someone has in their short-term forecast, the less you should listen to them. Many prognosticators will be more concerned with sounding right than making money. Even if they're right by chance, that doesn't mean they were giving you good advice. It means they got lucky. There are warning signs to look for, though. See Figure 9.1 for some of the words and phrases that

Always	I'm Not Wrong, the Market Is
Never	You *Have* to Buy This Right Now
I'm 100 Percent Certain	All the Upside, None of the Downside
It's a Sure Thing	Just Trust Me
Our Model Is a Black Box	I Can Promise You 20 Percent Annual Returns
We Never Lose Money	I'm Always Right

Figure 9.1   Words and Phrases to Watch Out for with Poor Financial Advice

are sure to grab your attention, but will rarely be found in legitimate, useful advice.

Beware of people who peddle investments that have increased substantially in price recently. More than likely these people missed the entire ride up and are trying to cash in while the gettin' is still good. It could be gold, real estate, stocks, whatever the investment du jour happens to be. It's much easier to jump on the bandwagon after an investment or asset class has shown huge gains. The same rings true for those who try to pile on asset classes that have fallen substantially in price. If there's been a huge increase or a huge decrease in an investment it's very easy to fall into the trap of extrapolating those moves into the future indefinitely. It's impossible to know for sure either way, because at the extremes sentiment takes over and no one can forecast investor emotions when they are at extremes.

Financial punditry is filled with perma-bulls and perma-bears. These people will do you no good, because to them, things are always unabashedly wonderful or colossally horrible with no in-between. There's no room for middle ground with these people as they always see the world through rose-colored glasses or the specter of an end to the financial system as we know it. Here are a few examples of these perma-arguers who somehow always turn the latest news or data point to fit their view of the world:

News: Oil prices are up.
Perma-Bulls: The economy is doing better.
Perma-Bears: Consumers have less discretionary spending.
News: Oil prices are down.
Perma-Bulls: Consumers get a boost in their pocketbook.
Perma-Bears: The economy is doing worse.
News: Economic growth is stagnating.
Perma-Bulls: Expectations are low.

> Perma-Bears: There's a huge disconnect between Wall Street and
>   Main Street.
> News: Economic growth is picking up.
> Perma-Bulls: Company profits should increase.
> Perma-Bears: The stock market is not the economy.

There are always going to be certain groups that can put a positive or negative spin on any piece of market-related data to fit their narrative. Don't give these people the time of day. Look for balanced viewpoints that look at both the potential rewards and the potential risks. What could go wrong? What is it that I'm not seeing? What are the risks I'm taking to get these potential rewards? It's an underrated trait to see both sides of a debate when giving advice. The best investors always think in terms of probabilities. Even if you're fairly certain of a particular outcome, always play devil's advocate to your own line of thinking to have a contingency plan in case something goes wrong.

Look for sources of information and advice that are willing to admit their mistakes. Self-awareness and humility are two attributes that are severely lacking in the advice-giving business. It's impossible to tell whether you're getting legitimate advice if the person avoids accountability for their recommendations.

Outsourcing to a Financial Professional

By now you should have a good handle on portfolio construction. You understand the importance of asset allocation and creating a comprehensive investment plan. You're well versed in the pitfalls of letting your emotions get in the way of making good decisions. What if you got to this point, but just don't think you have the emotional control, know-how, or time to be able to manage your investments on your own? There's no shame in admitting this fact. It makes perfect sense to seek the help of an experienced financial professional if this is the case. Admitting that you don't know everything is one of the first steps to becoming a better investor and decision maker. You just have to be able to determine what it is you should look for in a financial advisor or investment manager before making that decision.

There's no shame in outsourcing the important areas of your life. When you're sick, you go to a doctor. When you need legal advice you seek a reputable attorney. When your pipes burst you hire a plumber. These are all perfectly rational decisions because you're deferring to an expert. In outsourcing your investment decisions to a financial advisor, you're really making the decision to outsource your time, investment knowledge, and emotions. Unfortunately, those areas of expertise that I outlined—doctors, lawyers, and plumbers—all require more certification and training than someone needs to become a financial advisor. There are legitimate designations in financial planning—certified financial planner (CFP), portfolio management, chartered financial analyst (CFA)—that require a certain amount of time in the industry and comprehensive exams to be awarded, along with ongoing educational requirements. More than anything, a financial professional with the CFP or CFA designation has shown that they are committed to learning about their craft, which is always a good sign. But there are certainly people with those designations who don't give the best advice, as well as those who don't have them who give great advice. It's not as easy as just looking for a licensed professional. So you need to be aware of a few things as you seek out one of the most important hires you will ever make.

One of the first things to understand when thinking about finding a trustworthy financial advisor is that you will initially be attracted to the most confident, certain ones that you come across. In one experiment, investors tended to prefer financial advisors who made extreme, overconfident predictions as opposed to those who were more levelheaded. These people weren't necessarily judging these advisors by their process or investment ideas, but by how confident they were. People tend to assume that confidence is the same thing as being correct, which couldn't be further from the truth, These people's views become so clouded by overconfidence in their ability to do the impossible that they start to believe it.[1] There's nothing wrong with having conviction in your process, but it's a problem when that process becomes based exclusively about predicting the future instead of giving legitimate, long-term advice. No one is right all the time and the market has humbled even the most brilliant of investors who didn't have a heaping helping of humbleness.

While investors are attracted to certainty, hucksters are attracted to money. Having a large portfolio is a good problem to have, but it also brings out the scammers. The more money you have the larger the target on your back to get taken advantage of. In the classic Chris Farley movie *Tommy Boy*, Farley's character Tommy Callahan is trying to explain to a potential client the difference between the quality auto parts from his family's auto parts store, which have no guarantee on the box, and a competitor's auto parts that do have a guarantee on the box, but don't match Callahan's quality.

Tommy: Let's think about this for a sec, Ted. Why would somebody put a guarantee on a box? Hmmm, very interesting.
Ted Nelson (customer): Go on, I'm listening.
Tommy: Here's the way I see it, Ted. Guy puts a fancy guarantee on a box 'cause he wants you to feel all warm and toasty inside.
Ted Nelson: Yeah, makes a man feel good.
Tommy: Course it does. Why shouldn't it? Ya figure you put that little box under your pillow at night, the Guarantee Fairy might come by and leave a quarter, am I right, Ted?
Ted Nelson: What's your point?
Tommy: The point is, how do you know the fairy isn't a crazy glue sniffer? "Building model airplanes" says the little fairy; well, we're not buying it. He sneaks into your house once, that's all it takes. The next thing you know, there's money missing off the dresser, and your daughter's knocked up. I seen it a hundred times.
Ted Nelson: But why do they put a guarantee on the box?
Tommy: Because they know all they sold ya was a guaranteed piece of sh*t. That's all it is, isn't it? Hey, if you want me to take a dump in a box and mark it guaranteed, I will. I got spare time. But for now, for your customer's sake, for your daughter's sake, ya might wanna think about buying a quality product from me.

Any time a financial professional offers you a guarantee, think about *Tommy Boy*'s analogy. Anyone can offer 100 percent guarantees about the future because they make you feel all warm and fuzzy inside: "Sure, you can earn 20 percent a year with no downside risk. Just give me all of your hard-earned life savings." But that kind of guarantee is worthless. The best any financial professional can offer you is a high probability of success for meeting your goals.

Job number one for financial advisors is setting reasonable expectations, but you as the client have to reciprocate and set your own reasonable expectations about what it is they can do for you. You can't expect them to perform miracles. A good advisor should be able to

Table 9.1   Potential Value-Add from a Financial Advisor

Vanguard Advisor's Alpha Strategy Modules	Value-Add to Average Client Experience
Suitable asset allocation using broadly diversified funds/ETFs	>0%
Cost-effective implementation (expense ratios)	0.45%
Rebalancing	0.35%
Behavioral coaching	1.50%
Asset location	0% to 0.75%
Spending strategy (withdrawal order)	0% to 0.70%
Total return versus income investing	>0%
Potential value added	About 3%

Source: Vanguard.

do many things for you, but guaranteed market performance is not one of them.

What a Financial Advisor Can Do for You

Vanguard performed a comprehensive study that sought to quantify how much value a successful advisor could add to the performance of a client. They looked at a number of portfolio management issues and determined an amount that each could add to the client's bottom line relative to the average client experience. The conclusion was that improving upon each of those particular areas could add about 3 percent in net returns to the client, as you can see in Table 9.1. This is a huge performance number. You should notice that half of that 3 percent estimate in value-add, or 1.5 percent, comes from behavioral coaching. All of the other areas listed are important, but they will be all for naught if a financial advisor is unable to close the behavior gap. Client education, counseling, and setting reasonable expectations are the three pillars to this piece of the puzzle.[2]

This 3 percent figure shouldn't be thought of as an annual return number to add on top of your market performance year in and year out. That would be far too easy. The value-add is going to be sporadic. Most of the value will accrue during times of market stress or euphoria because that's when it's easy for investors to lose sight of their long-term plans. If your advisor is able to talk you down from the ledge when you're about to make a huge mistake, that's when they earn their fees and create value.

If you think an advisor can help improve your results and lower your stress level, a good starting point for what to look for is in this Vanguard list of value-added best practices. But you have to make sure that the advisor you choose actually focuses on these areas to help you reach your goals. If someone makes claims that they can add value in other areas, I would be skeptical.

In the spirit of keeping things simple, financial advisor and author Carl Richards has laid out three basic reasons to seek help from a financial advisor:

1. To help me clarify my goals.
2. To remind me of my goals.
3. To stand between me and stupid.[3]

Standing between you and stupid is what helps close the behavior gap (a phrase coined by Richards, actually). A good advisor should be better at forecasting your emotions and potential reactions than figuring out where the markets are heading. If they can talk you out of a few rotten decisions over the course of your relationship then they've done their job.

It's not enough to say they can do these things for you. An advisor has to be able to inform and show you how they will carry out a comprehensive financial plan on your behalf. They must be able to provide objective advice. They have to recommend suitable investments that make sense for your particular situation. It's also important to remember that a financial advisor is providing a service that you are paying for. They work for you, not the other way around. And while you can't make obscene demands, you absolutely must ask questions if you are confused or need more attention.

Behavior economist Meri Statman says that "Financial advisors frame themselves as *investment* managers, providers of 'beat-the-market' pills, when, in truth, they are mostly managers of investors." If you've gotten this far in the book you should understand this distinction. Not only does an advisor need to be an educator to their clients, but they are also something of a psychologist and emotional coach. They are there to manage your emotions, a somewhat odd relationship, but it's true. This is not an easy job, as we humans can be a tough bunch to understand. An advisor isn't there to simply choose investment products for you. Anyone can do that. In non-scientific terms, one of the most important jobs of a good advisor is cutting through the noise on behalf of their clients. They should be able to tell you two things:

1. These are the things you need to focus on and pay attention to.
2. These are the things you should ignore and pay no attention to.

Since ongoing education to the client is so important, that means the advisor must be continuously learning, as well. Most of the investment process comes down to thinking about thinking. If advisors aren't willing to put in the time to improve themselves, how can they be expected to improve your results? They should be selling a process, not a bunch of products. There's nothing inherently wrong with investment products. You do need them to build a portfolio. But your advisor should not just be a glorified salesperson.

A financial advisor should put your interests first when making investment decisions and recommendations. In finance terminology, they should be acting on your behalf as a fiduciary, meaning any time they offer advice they should first ask themselves, "Am I acting in the best interest of my client?" Advice should be based on evidence, not on the whims of their gut instincts. Advice should be given with a complete understanding of your entire financial ecosystem, not just your investment portfolio. You can't make informed decisions without a clear picture of someone's overall financial position including debts, spending habits, and future needs.

You'll need to know exactly how your advisor gets paid and what that fee will be, on both a percentage of assets basis, and a ballpark dollar amount based on the size of your portfolio. It's not a good sign if you find someone that's compensated based on commissions. Incentives matter, so you have to distinguish between someone selling you products versus giving solid advice and aligning their interests with yours. If a financial professional makes their money through commissions they are incentivized to churn your portfolio and sell you more and more products. That's not the type of advice that works for the client's interests.

You'll want to find someone who listens more than they talk. They should ask you plenty of questions and then spend their time explaining things when you turn the tables on them. They have to manage your portfolio using a well-thought-out process that includes the right asset allocation that suits your circumstances. And finally they need to lay out the policies that will guide their actions in the future to make sure the implementation process and ongoing maintenance of the portfolio are planned out in advance.

Getting things set up should be fairly painless. It's the implementation and ongoing maintenance of your financial plan that will cause you problems when it's someone else that's making the decisions on your behalf. In one experiment, whenever a broker gave accurate advice, clients reported that they felt less satisfaction than if they would have made the decision independently. It's more emotionally gratifying to make those calls yourself. It turns into something of a game. However if the same clients lost money, they felt much more regret than if the decision was theirs alone. So following someone else's recommendations reduces the emotional impact of losses. A financial professional can act as something of a shock absorber to your loss aversion. This is why people pay for investment advice. It's a way to defer not only your decisions, but your emotional state in the case of losses.[4]

Education should be a huge aspect of any financial advisor–client relationship. This cannot be overstated. If an advisor is ever going to be able to save you from yourself, first they must educate you. Not only do they have to tell you what to pay attention to or avoid, they also have to be able to figure things out about your situation that you're aware of, but you don't understand how important they are. Both analytical and good communication skills are essential for a successful financial advisor. You shouldn't need a translator to understand what they're saying. It should never be "Trust me, I'm the expert." It should be "Here's what I'm doing and here's why I'm doing it."

How to Be a Good Client

Investors want safety from losses during sell-offs, but all of the gains when the markets rise. They want to be tactical when the markets are volatile, but practice strict buy and hold during bull markets. Bonds are terrible investments during a stock bull market, but everyone clamors for them during a sell-off or recession. They want certainty and the ability to predict the future by switching to the best investments and asset classes before they take off, but to sidestep the poor performers before they begin to breakdown. Everyone wants to outperform the market over every single time frame, both short term and long term. There's a name for this strategy—it's called impossible.

Although the job of educator falls on the financial advisor, you still have an important role to play as a client. Appointing an advisor doesn't mean you can stop thinking about your finances all together. It just changes those areas that you really need to think strongly about. You can't outsource understanding and paying attention. Clients still have to know what's going on in their portfolio and with the markets. No one cares more about your money and what it represents than you. You are the biggest expert on your own situation and needs. That means speaking up and asking questions when you don't understand something or when you have concerns. You still have to stay involved in the process. Maybe the car is on cruise control but you're still steering it in the right direction.

You don't want to quibble over trivial details. It doesn't matter all that much if an advisor decides to put 12 percent of your portfolio into small-cap stocks instead of 15 percent. But your financial advisor should have a reasonable explanation for how your portfolio is constructed. Every asset class, fund, or security needs to have a thoughtful explanation attached as to why it deserves inclusion in your portfolio. Everything should be in there for a reason.

Advisors really need to help you get the big picture stuff right, which is why you need to know exactly what types of service you're getting—investment management, tax planning, estate management, and so on. You have to set expectations up front. What do you expect to get from this partnership and what does the advisor hope to get out of it? What are your biggest concerns and how will the advisor handle them? How will their process translate into your personal situation? How long will it take to get a portfolio up and running? Who are the third-party providers they work with (performance reports, bank custodians, tax prep, lawyers, etc.)? What's the rationale behind their investment approach? What's the portfolio rebalancing policy? What's the ongoing asset allocation plan? What determines buy and sell decisions? Basically, you have to be aware of what their investment guidelines are and how they'll apply to your portfolio. Gathering all of this information up front not only makes for an informed financial consumer, but it helps determine if an advisor is doing their job in the future.

Some other considerations when asking questions of a potential advisor: What are your biggest concerns? What are your experiences with the markets or financial advice in general? How can you turn my situation into a portfolio that will keep me on track? What are the total, all-inclusive fees for an average portfolio (including fund expense ratios and assets under management fees)? What securities or fund types do you use to build portfolios? What's the rationale behind the investment approach? What's your length of time working in the industry? What are your educational background and accreditations? Could you provide a current client as a reference?

Also, ask how they invest their personal money. It won't be exactly the same as clients because they, too, have their own personal circumstances, but the general message and approach should apply. Any advisor should have enough confidence in their own philosophy to utilize it themselves and eat their own cooking.

Your personal investment policy statement (IPS) should be in writing and clearly outline all of these issues. The written IPS gives you something to talk about at future meetings. It holds both parties accountable for their actions. The advisor should use the IPS to remind you of your plan of attack when short-term temptations creep in and you should use it to hold them accountable for what they said they were setting out to do.

Benchmarking and Ongoing Maintenance

Most investors assume that benchmarking is mainly for measuring performance against the indexes to compare over- and underperformance against the market. But in the advisor–client relationship, the main reason for measuring performance and benchmarking is to improve communication between the two parties. The purpose of performance measurement is not to provide answers. It's to help identify questions that investors and advisors should be looking into together. It can be the starting point for education to show clients what's contributing to or detracting from portfolio performance. Performance provides the narrative to communicate the advisor's ongoing process. Clients also have to consider the following for the implementation of the advisor relationship:

How will the relationship play out going forward once the portfolio is up and running?

How much communication will you need? Monthly reports?
Quarterly calls? Face-to-face meetings? Mostly online communication?

What's your learning style? How are you best educated?

How will they benchmark your portfolio and what risk metrics
will be shown?

How often do you meet or review your portfolio? What's the look
and detail of the periodic statements?

How is information exchanged?

You'll also want to judge your advisor over time. The best benchmark for an advisor is whether or not they do what they said they
would do for you. A good advisor absolutely must be able to explain
what it is they're going to do for you, but you have to make sure they
follow through with their promises. Did they do what they said they
were going to do? Did they follow through with the process that was
outlined? Or were they all talk and made the same mistakes you've
read about throughout this book? If they cannot fulfill their promises
for what they said they would do for you it's probably time to move
on. You might not agree with every move your financial advisor makes
for you, but they should make sense based on their process. Even
if it feels uncomfortable, you should rarely, if ever, be surprised by
their actions.

Alternatives

You probably need a healthy six-figure portfolio to find an advisor
who will work with you. There are now advisors who focus on smaller
client balances with lower minimums, but it's rare. For those who
really want to automate their plan and not have to do a ton of work,
the robo-advisors are a nice option. Companies like Wealthfront,
Betterment, Liftoff, and Charles Schwab will charge very low fees and
run a broadly diversified ETF portfolio that's fully automated. You
fill out a risk tolerance questionnaire and they perform such services
as tax-loss harvesting, rebalancing, and automatic contributions and
dividend reinvestments on your behalf. There's no emotional coaching that you would get from a traditional advisor, but it's a great place
to start, especially for younger investors with smaller portfolios. The

technology and services they are able to offer are only going to get better over time. It's still a young industry that should see plenty of growth and therefore competition. These are great services for those who can't meet the minimum balance requirements for traditional advisors or are only looking for automated portfolio management capabilities.

Key Takeaways from Chapter 9

- When vetting your sources of financial advice, look for self-awareness and humility, not certainty or guarantees about the future.
- Outsourcing to a financial advisor is intelligent behavior if you don't have the time, expertise, or emotional control to implement an ongoing financial plan.
- Education and emotional coaching from an advisor are even more important than portfolio management.
- Both parties have to set reasonable expectations in the client–advisor relationship.

Notes

1. Paul Price and Eric Stone, "Intuitive Evaluation of Likelihood Judgment Producers: Evidence for a Confidence Heuristic," *Journal of Behavioral Decision Making*, December 2003.
2. Francis M. Kinniry Jr., Colleen M. Jaconetti, Michael A. DiJoseph, and Yan Zilbering, "Putting a Value on Your Value: Quantifying Vanguard Advisor's Alpha," Vanguard, March 2014, https://advisors.vanguard .com/iwe/pdf/ISGQVAA.pdf.
3. Carl Richards (@behaviorgap), tweet, May 24, 2013.
4. Richard Peterson, *Inside the Investor's Brain: The Power of Mind Over Money* (Hoboken, NJ: John Wiley & Sons, 2007).

Conclusion

Before setting out to write this book I sought out some of my favorite financial authors and thinkers to ask for advice on how to approach the book writing process and what to include in its contents. One of the best pieces of advice I received was very simple and common sense in its message. This person told me to ask myself the following question before writing this book:

> Imagine that your grandmother came to you and wanted to know ten things about investing that she could understand and that she needs to understand. What would you tell her?

I love this advice because it dovetails nicely with the way Warren Buffett writes his famous annual shareholder letters that have taught me so much about investing over the years. When asked by a group of MBA students about his writing style, Buffett said, "In my first draft, I address it to my sisters who don't know a lot about finance. 'Dear sisters'—I explain to them what they would want to know in their position. I also like to write one section that is a general teaching lesson that doesn't directly apply to Berkshire."[1] Buffett gets more praise than anyone for his investment prowess, but I think he's actually underrated in his ability to explain complex topics about the markets and investing in a language a wide audience can understand. That was my goal here as well.

In the spirit of keeping things simple and understandable, here are 10 things about investing that I would tell my grandmother that I think are important for her to understand to sum up the entire message of this book:

1. **Less is more.** It is possible that if you put in the extra time and effort that you could consistently earn market-beating returns over time using a more complex, active investment strategy? Of course. Anything is possible. But the beauty of a simple

investment plan is that it can allow you to reach your goals *and* live your life. Wealth is nothing without meaning attached to it. Time is often the most valuable commodity and if utilizing a simple investment approach gives you more time to spend with loved ones doing the things you love to do, then that's a huge benefit that can't be quantified by any benchmark.

Plus, making fewer decisions in the investment process reduces the chances that decision fatigue from a lack of willpower will ruin your plan by making unforced errors.

Action Steps:
Cut away the fat from your portfolio and process. Start by minimizing the numbers of funds or holdings that make up your portfolio. Get rid of anything you don't understand or don't have a good reason for holding.

2. **Focus on what you can control.** There are so many factors that affect the financial markets and your individual investments that's it's probably impossible to list them all. Just remember that the majority of these factors are completely out of your control. It doesn't matter how much you worry about them because it won't make a difference one way or another. Too many investors take things personally when the markets or a particular investment go against them. The market will never have a vendetta against you. Focusing only on those areas that are within your control—creating a comprehensive investment plan, setting a reasonable asset allocation, understanding your risk profile and time horizon, and reducing crippling errors—is one of the best ways to reduce or eliminate many of the emotions that plague so many investors and cause harmful mistakes at the wrong time.

Action Steps:
Go through your portfolio and investment process. Write down each step in your process and focus only on those areas that are within your control. Feel free to stay interested in anything else that doesn't make the list, but never let it affect your portfolio decisions.

3. **The best investment process is the one you are willing and able to stick with through any market cycle.** It really doesn't matter what kind of strategy you employ if you can't see it through

a number of different market and economic environments. Everyone is tested at times. It's going to happen. Structure your process to account for this fact and your own personality and emotions. A rules-based investment plan can help investors stay disciplined, but a plan can't do it on its own. You have to stay out of your own way and follow through, as well. Automate as many good decisions up front as you can to avoid having to make huge moves during times of market stress and emotional duress.

Action Steps:
Be completely honest with yourself. Look back on some of the worst investment decisions you've made in the past. Now figure out how to structure your process so you never make the same mistakes again in the future. There's no shame in making mistakes. That's going to happen. The worst results come from investors who make the same mistakes over and over again without learning from them.

4. **Emotional intelligence and an understanding of behavioral biases are much more important than the level of your IQ.** A successful investor knows how to combine the correct balance between risk and reward with a deep understanding of financial market history and a well-thought-out, evidence-based portfolio of financial assets. But all of these pieces of the puzzle are worthless without the correct temperament and common sense to understand yourself and human nature. Some of the most intelligent people on Wall Street blow up their portfolios because they aren't equipped with the self-awareness and humility to keep their ego and overconfidence in check. Yes, intelligence is important, but only up to a certain point. There are plenty of smart people working in the financial industry, but there are very few who have the ability to control their emotions. You must not only understand your own areas of weakness, but also how the crowd can lose their collective minds, as we've seen throughout history.

Action Steps:
From your list of mistakes from above, figure out which behavioral biases contributed to each. Next, work on automating good decisions up front through a sound, systematic

investment process so you don't have to worry about allowing them to interfere with future decisions.

5. **You're not the next David Swensen, but that's okay.** Extraordinary market returns are reserved for a small percentage of the world's greatest investors, many of whom have advantages you will never be able to replicate. Letting go of this pipe dream is the first step towards becoming a better investor. You don't have to try for extraordinary because above average performance can put you far ahead of your peers and some of the largest professional investment funds, as we've seen throughout the book.

Passive, systematic, repeatable investment strategies are the best option for the majority of investors. A small number of active managers can and do outperform the markets. You just have a higher probability of success with index funds and ETFs than you do by trying to choose the small number of active funds that consistently outperform.

Action Steps:
Look in the mirror. Do you see Warren Buffett? If not, don't try for the same type of performance that Buffett has earned over the years. Instead, take his long-term outlook to heart and focus on improving your emotional intelligence.

6. **Stock picking is sexier, but asset allocation is much more important for your overall performance and risk tolerance.** Asset allocation—your mix of stocks, bonds, cash, and other investments within your portfolio—is an often overlooked aspect of the investing process that should not be taken lightly. While not perfect, a diversified asset allocation approach over longer time horizons gives investors a high probability for success if they're willing to stay with it over time.

Diversified portfolios aren't really meant to manage volatility, although that is often a byproduct of diversification. They're really meant to manage your emotions. This does not mean your portfolio won't go down or participate in a market crash if you are exposed to those markets. It's more about giving up on home runs and strikeouts to accept walks and singles.

Risk management is something that gets brushed aside every time there is a bull market. No one wants to diversify. Everyone wants to own only the best market, sector, or stocks that are outperforming. These feelings should be short-lived, because the outperformance of any one area of the market will be as well. Asset allocation, diversification, periodic rebalancing, and the discipline to see your plan through, while not exciting, are some of the best risk controls you have as an investor.

Action Steps:
Look at your current asset allocation between stocks, bonds, cash and other assets. Does this allocation match your risk profile and time horizon? If not, fix it now. Don't wait.

7. **Get rich patiently and never be in a hurry.** Saving money will always trump the best investment strategy. Even if you are able to deliver extraordinary investment performance like the all-time great investors, it wouldn't matter towards building your capital base if you aren't a diligent saver. This means that saving should be priority number one before all else in your investment plan. While dollar cost averaging is a simple strategy that has its pros and cons, it's not only a form of risk and emotional management, but it's also very practical, since you can save directly from every periodic paycheck you receive. Automating the saving process is one of the best ways to build a nest egg over time since the decision is taken out of your hands.

   The most comfortable financial advice will always be short-term oriented. Uncomfortable advice is typically long-term in nature. You're going to have to make uncomfortable decisions occasionally to avoid making the big mistake that could lead to irreversible risks. High-frequency traders (HFT) try to arbitrage extremely short-term moves in stocks, often in fractions of a second. That's not the game you want to get into because you cannot compete at that level. Long-term investing is something that Wall Street can never arbitrage away. Time arbitrage is therefore one of the biggest edges you have as an investor. Don't take it lightly, as long-term returns are the only ones that matter.

Action Steps:
Figure out what "long-term" means for you and your specific goals. You'll likely have a number of different uses for your savings, so determine what the particular time horizon is for each and keep that in mind when making investment decisions.

If you're not reaching your savings goals set up a monthly transfer to be automatically deducted from your paycheck. Then increase that amount over time every time you receive a raise. That way you'll never notice the money is even missing, reducing the effects of loss aversion.

8. **You cannot expect to make money in the stock market without losing money on occasion.** Since 1928, on average, stocks have fallen at least 5 percent three times a year, at least 10 percent once a year, at least 20 percent once every four years, and at least 30 percent once every decade. Oh, and on four separate occasions stocks have been cut in half or more. Yet in that time your money would have doubled every seven and a half years. On an inflation-adjusted basis, it would have doubled every decade. This is the conundrum investors are forced to deal with. The reason stocks make money over the long term is because they have to ability to go down in the short term. As John Maynard Keynes once said, "I should say that it is from time to time the duty of a serious investor to accept the depreciation of his holdings with equanimity and without reproaching himself. An investor should be aiming primarily at long-period results, and should be solely judged by these."

This is why it's so important to understand your ability and willingness to take risk. Allocate more money to less volatile investments if you can't handle losses, but understand that you will likely have to save more to reach your financial goals if you carry a risk-averse portfolio. There's no way you can avoid risk in the financial markets if you hope to beat inflation over the long term and earn a respectable return on your portfolio. Stocks outperform bonds over longer cycles, but bonds provide stability when you need it the most. Bonds feel safer to investors after a crash while stocks feel riskier. We are thrilled when every other purchase we make in life goes on sale, but not so with our investments.

Without a long time horizon, performance in the markets can be quite messy. Build your portfolio and mindset accordingly. Successful investing can be painful over shorter time frames but beautiful over longer ones.

Action Steps:
Before the next market crash (not after) determine how much you can stand to lose both financially and psychologically. Never have more money in stocks than you can stand to lose. It will only lead to poor decisions at the wrong time.

9. **Simplicity, discipline, patience, and a focus on the long-run are generally lacking in the financial industry.** These traits are your edge. As the world around you will only get faster and more instantaneous, there will be the temptation to make snap decisions without thinking about the consequences. The default to an act-first, think-later mindset is becoming pervasive. This is especially true in the financial markets, where investors have been migrating towards short-termism for years. Avoid this line of thinking at all costs. Professional investors are finding it much harder to utilize long-term thinking as they're being judged on shorter and shorter time frames, but individual investors have no one to answer to but themselves. Take advantage of this by structuring a disciplined investment plan to take into account your specific time horizons. And think long-term process over short-term outcomes to increase your chances of succeeding over the long haul.

Risk management should always trump chasing short-term performance. One of the best ways to control risk in a portfolio is to understand exactly what you own and why you own it. How do your asset classes typically behave? What types of securities are in your portfolio? This is why simplicity is such a useful form of risk control. It's much harder to be surprised by what you hold in your portfolio at any time.

Action Steps:
Do you have an investment plan? In writing? That covers all of your goals and desires? If not, make it a priority, keep it simple and figure out how to force yourself to think and act for the long-term by avoiding short-term behavior.

10. **Wealth means nothing if there's no meaning attached to it.**
Nick Murray once said, "No matter how much money you
have, if you're still worried, you aren't wealthy."[2] At the end
of the day, wealth only matters to the extent that you can
use it to increase your happiness and fulfillment in life. In
the book *Happy Money: The Science of Smarter Spending*, authors
Elizabeth Dunn and Michael Norton performed a battery of
tests to determine how one could increase their happiness by
spending money. They found five different ways to do this:

1. Buy experiences.
2. Make it a treat.
3. Buy time.
4. Pay now, consume later.
5. Invest in others.

Interestingly enough, the spending choice that has the
biggest effect on a person's happiness is how much money
they spend on others. Study after study shows that the more
people invest in others, the happier they are. It's not necessarily huge amounts of cash either. Even donating small amounts
puts people in a better mood. Dunn and Norton found that
donating money to charity had a comparable effect to dou-
bling household income on levels of happiness.[3] Building
wealth through an investment portfolio is not about hoard-
ing money, but about finding meaning for your money.

Investing, in its most basic form, is about delaying gratification today, to experience gratification in the future. You
have to think long and hard about the uses for your money
when you begin the wealth-building process.

Action Steps:
Don't make it all about the money. Attach meaning to your
portfolio to keep your eyes on the real prize. Figure out how
your money can make you happier and find ways to enjoy it.

Book List

While there's no substitute for experience in the markets, the majority of my learning about investing and the history of the financial

markets comes from reading books. These are some of my favorites that have taught me plenty over the years.

Simple Wealth, Inevitable Wealth by Nick Murray
Your Money and Your Brain by Jason Zweig
Thinking, Fast and Slow by Daniel Kahneman
The Four Pillars of Investing by William Bernstein
The Little Book of Common Sense Investing by John Bogle
The Little Book of Behavioral Investing by James Montier
Stocks for the Long Run by Jeremy Siegel
The Warren Buffett Portfolio by Robert Hagstrom
Damn Right: Behind the Scenes with Berkshire Hathaway Billionaire Charlie Munger by Janet Lowe
Investing: The Last Liberal Art by Robert Hagstrom
Success Equation: Untangling Skill and Luck in Business, Sports, and Investing by Michael Mauboussin
Devil Take the Hindmost by Edward Chancellor
The Most Important Thing by Howard Marks
All About Asset Allocation by Rick Ferri
Winning the Loser's Game by Charles Ellis

Notes

1. David Kass, "Warren Buffett's Meeting with University of Maryland MBA Students," *University of Maryland*, November 15, 2013, http://blogs.rhsmith.umd.edu/davidkass/uncategorized/warren-buffetts-meeting-with-university-of-maryland-mbams-students-november-15-2013/.
2. Nick Murray, *Simple Wealth, Inevitable Wealth* (New York: Nick Murray Company, 2004).
3. Elizabeth Dunn and Michael Norton, *Happy Money: The Science of Smarter Spending* (New York: Simon & Schuster, 2014).

About the Author

Ben Carlson, CFA, has spent his entire career managing institutional portfolios for pensions, endowments, and foundations. He is also the creator and author of the blog *A Wealth of Common Sense.*

Index